J. L. Pickering

Souvenir of the Illinois Legislature

J. L. Pickering

Souvenir of the Illinois Legislature

ISBN/EAN: 9783744679114

Printed in Europe, USA, Canada, Australia, Japan

Cover: Foto ©ninafisch / pixelio.de

More available books at **www.hansebooks.com**

PRICE, $3.   PAPER, $1.

SOUVENIR

OF THE

ILLINOIS LEGISLATURE

OF 1893.

Over 200 Portraits, with Biographical Sketches of Every Member of the General Assembly, State Officers, and The Press.

Also Engravings of the Senate and House Chambers, the Capitol, the Executive Mansion, the Lincoln Home, Hotels, Etc.

"Be not afraid of greatness:
Some are born great, some achieve
greatness and some have greatness thrust upon them."

Copyright, 1893, by J. L. Pickering.

SPRINGFIELD:
PRESS OF THE ILLINOIS STATE JOURNAL.

A Question of Personal Privilege:

This Souvenir is dedicated to the gentlemen whose portraits appear. It has been no easy task to assemble so many statesmen under one standard. Nor has it been easy to select good photographs, have them engraved and printed so handsomely as has been done.

I am sincerely grateful for the encouragement and aid rendered by those whose comely faces follow this page. Nor am I unmindful of the confidence reposed in me by my friends.

Almost all the photos were obtained from the popular gallery of L. S. Anderson, Springfield, although many were furnished by Halliday & Kessberger, also of Springfield, and they do their own talking. The printing was done in Springfield by The State Journal Company, and will bear the most critical inspection. The engravings are all on rolled copper, and were made by Blomgren Bros. & Co., Chicago, who have added to their reputation.

Trusting that those who complimented me by their preference will not regret it, and hoping that all will return two years hence, I beg to submit my report without further comment.

Sincerely,

J. L. PICKERING.

Springfield, March, 1893.

JOHN P. ÁLTGELD,
Governor of Illinois.

THE GOVERNOR.

It is an honor to be the chief executive over four millions of people. It is a greater honor to be chosen chief executive under the peculiar conditions that maintained during the fierce campaign of 1892 in Illinois. Illinois was admitted to the Union in 1818, and immediately its sparse population decided almost unanimously for the principles of Jefferson and Madison and Monroe. There was no break in the phalanx of democratic victories from that time until '56, when a combination of slavery, knownothingism and restlessness at the arrogance of democratic leaders turned the state over to the Republicans—which party almost immediately after the election absorbed the majority of the "American" element, which was a considerable factor in the campaign of '56. Buchanan's electors carried the state, also. From that day to Jan. 10, 1893, there was no serious break in the republican column, except in '62. To be sure the legislature was democratic until '65, and a fusion with the greenbackers enabled them to elect a superintendent of public instruction in '74. But for over thirty years Illinois was set down as good for 25,000 to 50,000 republican plurality. The result of last fall's election dazed republicans and democrats. While Michigan, Iowa, Kansas, Wisconsin, Ohio and other rockbound republican states had at times wandered from the path of republicanism, it was believed that nothing could affect Illinois.

And so the democrats entered the campaign of '92 without hope. Gov. John P. Altgeld expected to be elected, and those nearest him predicted it with confidence. The energy, ability and talent for organization, possessed by the democratic candidate for governor in a great measure decided the contest. Judge Altgeld's promise to the convention that his "would be a strictly business administration," if elected, is being carried out. He is a business man who applies business principles in the discharge of his official duties. And he demands qualifications other than party service—although that is also necessary—from the men he appoints to office. He has filled the more important places with men who will carry out his policy, and the press has generally endorsed them.

John P. Altgeld was born in Prussia in 1848, and came to this country with his parents when a boy, the father settling on a farm near Mansfield, Ohio. At this early date he began to show those studious traits and mental powers that have since raised him to eminence. He worked hard and studied his books when he could steal a few minutes. He attended the schools when work on the farm was not pressing, and at the age of 16 enlisted in Co. C, 164th O. Inf., and went to the front, participating in the campaign of Grant that closed the war. Returning home he spent the next few years alternately teaching school, studying and working as a farm hand. Then he went west to St. Louis where he read law in a desultory way; and afterwards in the office of Haven & Rea, Savannah, Mo. His industry and faculty for diving to the heart of his subject brought clients, fame and prosperity. In '74 he was elected prosecuting attorney of Andrew county, but in October, '75, he resigned his office, sold his furniture and moved to Chicago. He took little interest in politics for several years, but in '84 ran for congress in an overwhelming republican district. He was defeated, but cut down the republican majority. In '86 without solicitation on his part he was nominated for superior judge of Cook county, at that time about 12,000 republican. He hesitated some time before accepting, but finally did so, and so thorough a canvass did he make, and so perfect was his organization, that notwithstanding defections from the democratic party and quarrels within the ranks, he was elected by a large majority, the laboring men being especially active in his interest. A multiplicity of private interests compelled him to resign his place on the bench in August, '91. He has become quite wealthy, principally by shrewd buying and selling of real estate in Chicago, a proper field for a man with capital and sharp business instinct. He also has been interested in street railways in various cities. He was nominated for governor on the first ballot in the democratic convention in April, '92, and made two hard canvasses of the state—one a preliminary trip in which he visited every county to learn the conditions, and give instructions for organization, and another to address the people on the issues of the day. In '78 he married Miss Emma Ford, an accomplished lady who has already become very popular in Springfield society.

THE LIEUTENANT GOVERNOR.

Joseph B. Gill, President of the Senate and Lieutenant Governor, served two terms in the house in '89 and '91 and was nominated on the first ballot in April, '92, for lieutenant governor by the democratic state convention. He was born on a farm near Marion, Williamson county, Feb. 17, 1862, and is the youngest lieutenant governor ever elected in this state. In '63 his family moved to De Soto, Jackson county, and in '68 to Murphysboro, where he has lived ever since. He was educated in the public schools, at the Christian Brothers College in St. Louis, and at the Southern Illinois Normal, at Carbondale, graduating from the latter in June, '84. Then he completed a law term of two years at Ann Arbor, graduating in July, '86, and was admitted to the Michigan bar, passing an examination before the supreme and circuit courts of that state. He never practiced his profession, but returning home engaged in newspaper work, buying an interest in the Murphysboro Independent, which he conducted and edited up to Jan. 1, '93.

About the first office he asked from his party was to the house in '88 and it was given him, also a return for faithful services in '90. In both general assemblies he was a strong anti-corporation man, and championed the cause of the laboring people on every measure that came up of interest to them. He was instrumental in securing the passage of the gross weight bill, the weekly pay bill, the anti-truck store bill, and did all he could to advance the arbitration bill to a successful issue. His efforts to benefit a class of people who have few friends in the legislature, were appreciated, and soon after the legislature of '91 adjourned, there was a demand for him to go on the state ticket. Resolutions were adopted in many lodges and unions commending Gov. Gill to the democratic state convention and urging his nomination. An unusual interest was taken in his election because of the close relations between the candidate and the class whose cause he had championed in the legislature. He was triumphantly elected, running ahead of most of his colleagues on the Democratic state ticket. He is an impartial presiding officer, and has won the respect of the senators already.

THE SECRETARY OF STATE.

William H. Hinrichsen, Secretary of State, was born in Franklin, Ill., May 27, 1850, and educated at the Illinois University. His father was born in the Grand Duchy of Mecklenberg, and emigrated to America when a boy. His mother was born in Morgan county, and her father, who was a soldier of the war of 1812, came from Virginia. After leaving the University Mr. Hinrichsen entered the office of the general stock agent of the Wabash railroad, remaining for four years and resigning to become deputy sheriff of Morgan county in '74. He was there for three terms, and was elected sheriff in '80. Two years later he bought an interest in The Evening Courier with Geo. E. Doying, and declining a renomination for sheriff, he entered the newspaper business with vigor. He edited The Courier until '86, when the firm purchased The Quincy Daily Herald, and he went over to take charge of it. He soon raised it to the front rank among provincial dailies, and made its influence as a democratic organ felt all over western Illinois. In '90 The Herald was sold and Mr. Hinrichsen returned to Jacksonville to resume editorial charge of The Courier, but the democratic caucus in Jan. '91 chose him by acclamation for clerk of the house, and after the legislature adjourned he entered into the work of the campaign of '92 with his usual vigor and discretion. As a member of the executive committee of the state committee, he made a careful canvass of every county in the state, paving the way by an intelligent observation of the condition of the party and suggestions as to organization, for the sweeping triumph of '92. He was named

for secretary of state on first ballot. He had charge of the press bureau during the campaign. When he was 21 he was elected justice of the peace in a strong republican precinct. He has been a delegate to every democratic state convention since he was old enough to vote. He has been a member, and chairman or secretary most of the time, of the Morgan and Adams county committees since he reached the voting age. He was on the executive committee of the state committee during the campaign of '90, and resigned when nominated for secretary of state. In '73 he married Miss Louise Sparks, and has two sons and one daughter.

THE STATE TREASURER.

An epitome of the life of Rufus N. Ramsay, State Treasurer, will contain no failures as a politician and no scars as a servant of the people. His life has been that of an honorable and industrious gentleman who accepts office as a duty, and who discharges his official responsibilities with fidelity, honesty and energy. Popular, of course, for he always ran ahead of his ticket. As a member of the house in '89 and '91 he was a safe leader, with a strong following of the best element. He saw the objectionable features in the compulsory education law of '89, and was denied the privilege of explaining his vote by the house. He did say during the confusion and objections that he was a friend of compulsory education, but the present bill possessed several objectionable features, and he could not vote for it. He is a quiet, unostentatious man, shrewd as a politician, and a tireless worker.

Rufus N. Ramsay was born on a Clinton county farm May 20, 1838, and spent three years at Illinois College, some time at McKendree, and graduated from the State University at Bloomington, Ind., in '64. Then he studied law with Gov. French and also with Judge Underwood at Belleville; admitted to the bar in '65, and practiced for several years in Carlyle. He gradually became interested in farm lands and real estate, and quit the law at a time when he had a large and lucrative practice. In '70 the banks of Ramsay & Seiter, of Carlyle, and Seiter & Ramsay, of Lebanon, were organized and prospered until '80, when the partnership was dissolved, the resident partner in each city tak-

ing complete control. He was elected county clerk in '65 when every county officer was a republican, and was re-elected. He has done as much or more than any other one man to make Clinton county democratic by 900 to 1,100. He is a Presbyterian. In '64 he married Miss Julia Toney, and has two daughters and one son. Is largely interested in farm lands and Chicago and St. Louis real estate. His father, who came to Illinois in '16 from South Carolina, is strong and vigorous at 88, and was in Springfield inauguration day. He is the oldest democrat in the state, and a man whose whole life has been above reproach.

SUPERINTENDENT OF SCHOOLS.

There have been few democrats in the office of Superintendent of Public Instruction of the state of Illinois since 1857, when the republicans took control of the state government. In fact Henry Raab, of Belleville, is the only democrat that has ever been elected to the office on a straight party platform and ticket. He was elected in '82 by about 3,000 plurality. The state went republican by 40,000 in '80. He declined a renomination in '86 but in vention, but it was discouraged by Mr. Raab, who has little taste for political life.

Henry Raab was born in Wetzlar, Rhenish Prussia, June 20, 1837. He was educated in the Kindergarten, public school and Royal Gymnasium of his native city; also by private tutors. After leaving school he learned the trade of a currier in his father's shops and emigrated to the United States in '53, finding work at his trade in Cincinnati. The year following he went to St. Louis and later on to Belleville, where he was for a time en-

was named against his will and was elected by a plurality of over 34,000 running far ahead of the ticket.

In his capacity of superintendent of public instruction he took a firm stand for the better supervision of schools and the better education of teachers. He discharged his duties in a quiet unostentatious manner, yet with an energy and ability that made him many friends among the school teachers and educators in the state. At the close of his first administration he returned to Belleville to superintend the public schools of that city. His name was urged in many quarters for governor before the last democratic state con-
gaged in clerking. During all this time he was a close student of political and economic questions, and in '57 became a teacher in the public schools of Belleville. In '60 he was elected librarian of the St. Clair county library, an office which he held until '83, when the city of Belleville assumed control of that institution. In the teaching profession he rose to be a principal, and in '73 was made city superintendent of schools of Belleville, which office he held until he was elected superintendent of public instruction in '82. In '59 he was married to Miss Mathilde Von Lengerken, and has one son and two daughters.

THE ATTORNEY-GENERAL.

Maurice T. Maloney, Attorney-General, was born in County Kerry, Ireland, July 26, 1849. After a thorough course in the common schools he entered Listowel Seminary, graduating in the classical course. He moved to America in '67, and began a course of study in moral philosophy in the Niagara Falls Seminary of Our Lady of Angels. Afterwards he studied theology in Wheeling, and taught school for a time in Wytheville, Va.

election he has commenced suit against Ex-Auditors Lippincott, Swigert and Pavey and their bondsmen to recover fees alleged to be illegally diverted and retained.

Although he has been in office less than three months at this writing Mr. Moloney has rendered several opinions of great importance. And the best legal talent as well as the great newspapers—republican and democratic—agree with his conclusions. The opinion in regard to the right of the canal commissioners of the Illinois & Michigan Canal to turn over to the trustees

In '69 he entered the University of Virginia, near Charlottesville, founded by Thomas Jefferson, from which he graduated in '71 with the Bachelor of Laws degree. He then moved to Ottawa, Ill., where he has since lived and had a very successful practice.

He was city attorney of Ottawa for four years, states attorney of LaSalle county from '84 to '88, and prosecuted all the boodlers, recovering some $50,000 for the county. He was legal advisor to the board of supervisors for seven years. He was nominated for attorney-general in the democratic state convention in '92 on the first ballot with four candidates. Since his

of the Chicago Drainage District a portion of the canal for sanitary purposes, is probably the most important one. Important, also, are his carefully prepared views on the right of the state auditor to retain a part of the fees from the insurance companies; in regard to the right of the auditor to employ a Chicago attorney, and in regard to treasurers loaning public funds.

He is a man of indomitable energy, and has made a very favorable impression already on the people of the state. In 1873 he married Miss Annie J. Graham, of Ottawa, and has five children—three sons and two daughters.

THE ADJUTANT-GENERAL.

Gen. Alfred Orendorff, Adjutant General of the state of Illinois, was born July 29, 1845, in Logan county, and was educated at the Wesleyan University, Bloomington, and the military school at Fulton, Illinois. In '66 Gen. Orendorff graduated from the Albany, N. Y., Law School, with the degree of Bachelor of Laws. He began practice in Springfield in '67 with the firm of Herndon & Zane. The firm was successively Herndon & Orendorff and Orendorff & Creighton. When Judge Creighton was elected to the circuit bench, he formed a partnership with Robert H. Patton, under the firm name of Orendorff & Patton, which still exists, and is one of the strongest in Central Illinois.

Originally he was a republican, he took the first step towards democracy in '72, when so many republicans of liberal views joined the struggling party of the common people. In '72 he was a delegate to the democratic national convention, and heartily favored the nomination of Judge Lyman Trumbull for president. In '73 he was nominated by the liberals and ratified by the democrats, for the Illinois house, and was elected. He took an active part as a member of the judiciary committee in revising the laws of the state in conformity with the constitution of '70. He has been chairman of the democratic state committee for several years, and was delegate to several national democratic conventions. In '82 as candidate for state treasurer he pulled a republican majority of 40,000 down to about 5,000, and four years later he made another splendid run for the same office. He is vice president of the German-Amer-

ican Loan association and of the Franklin Life Insurance company of this city, and has large interests in real estate. He has held the highest offices within the gift of the Odd Fellows; has been representative to the sovereign grand lodge of the world every year since 1880. In 1870 he married Julia, the daughter of Col. John Williams, one of the wealthiest and most respected pioneers of Illinois, and has two daughters and one son. He was appointed adjutant-general by Gov. Altgeld Jan. 20, 1893, an appointment that was most cordially received in every quarter of the state, as well as elsewhere where he is known.

SUPREME COURT REPORTER.

The oldest Supreme Court Reporter in the United States is Norman L. Freeman, of Illinois, and there is none more accurate or more satisfactory to the lawyers and judges. The position is one of peculiar difficulty, and requires qualifications above that of a lawyer, or even a judge. Indeed, Illinois lawyers frequently quote the syllabus of a supreme court decision in preference to the words of the justice. Judge Freeman has a happy faculty possecrets of the court. He has a handsome home in Springfield, and is a democrat of the old school.

Norman L. Freeman was born in Caledonia, Livingston Co., N. Y., May 9, 1823. His parents, Truman and Hannah (Dow) Freeman, trace their ancestry back to the early pioneers. In '31 he accompanied his widowed mother to Ann Arbor, and six years later they moved to Detroit. He worked in his brother's store in Cleveland for a time, and in '40 entered an academy in that city. From there he went to the Ohio University, at Athens,

sessed by few men, of extracting the kernel from the shell of a decision, and painting it in short terse sentences. It is this that renders him so valuable in his capacity of reporter of the supreme court, and makes his reports models of excellence and reliability. He has edited and published 106 volumes of Illinois Reports, embodying over 7,000 cases. He is the personification of courtesy and accommodation. By nature of his office he is close to the justices of the court. No doubt he has been approached many times by interested litigants for information in regard to pending cases, but he was never known to violate the sacred and had for fellow students S. S. Cox and Milton Latham. In '43 he moved to Kentucky and taught school to pay his expenses while studying law. In '46 he began the practice of his profession in Morganfield, Ky. The great struggle between the north and south compelled him to move to a more peaceful state than Kentucky, for he inherited many Quaker principles from his mother's family. In '62 he moved to Shawneetown, and in April '63, was appointed reporter of the supreme court, and has held the office ever since. In December, '49, he married Miss Tranquilla Richeson, and has four children—a son and three daughters.

SUPREME-APPELLATE COURTS.

The state of Illinois was divided half a century ago into three grand divisions of the supreme court. The seat of the Central Grand Division is located at Springfield.

E. A. SNIVELY.

ETHAN A. SNIVELY, Clerk of the Supreme Court, Central Grand Division, was born in Cuba, Fulton, Co., Ill., Feb. 17, 1845, and received a common school education. In '60 he entered the office of The Squatter Sovereign, at Havana, to learn the printing business. Before he was 21 years old he assumed editorial and business management of The Rushville Times, and conducted the paper for over two years. In July, '68 he began the publication of The Galesburg Times, and for nearly a year he preached radical democracy in a county that gave nearly 3,000 republican majority. Then he edited The Pekin Register for a few months, resigning in the fall of '69 to become city editor of The Peoria Daily National Democrat. In Oct. '71 he assumed control of The Macoupin Enquirer at Carlinville, which he conducted until April, '77, when he relinquished it and engaged in the agricultural implement business. In '79 he assumed editorial control of The Macoupin Herald at Carlinville, and in '80 this paper was consolidated with The Enquirer, which he edited until '83, when he sold it. In '78 he was elected clerk of the supreme court, and was re-elected in '84 and '90 by increased majorities, the last two times having no opposition in the democratic convention. He was president of the Illinois Press Association in '79 and '80, and is a very active honorary member now. The first work he did in a printing office was to assist in getting out an extra on Sunday—announcing the first nomination of Abraham Lincoln for president. There were few railroads and no telegraph in the west then, and it took three days for the news to reach Havana.

The Appellate Court, Third District, comprises the same counties as Central Grand Division, Supreme Court; it was organized in '77; the present incumbent is the first clerk elected by the people.

GEORGE W. JONES, Clerk of the Appellate Court, Third District, came to Illinois with his parents when a child and was raised at Griggsville and in Pike county, one of the most fertile and beautiful counties in the state. He received a good common school education, and was clerk of the circuit court of Pike county from '60 to '64, and '72 to '76. He also held several minor offices, member of the board of supervisors, the board of education, etc. In '78 he was elected clerk of the appellate court, and was re-elected in '84 and '90 by increased majorities; was nominated by acclamation in the democratic convention in '84-'90. He is a strong democrat,

GEO. W. JONES.

and an enthusiastic Cleveland man. In '50 he was married to Miss Celia Bennett, of Marshall Co., Ill., and has two sons—Frank H., member of the last house of representatives and a promising young attorney of Springfield, and Fred. B., of the Adams & Westlake Manufacturing Co., Chicago.

THE RAILROAD COMMISSION.

Probably the most important board attached to the state administration is the Railroad and Warehouse Commission, organized in 1870. It is composed of three members, who draw $3,500

WM S. CANTRELL.

each per annum, and expenses, and a secretary at $2,500. Term of office two years; Gov. Altgeld appointed the present board Jan. 23, '93, and they were immediately confirmed by the senate. The board consists of Wm. S. Cantrell, of Benton, Charles F. Lape of Springfield and Thomas Gahan of Chicago, with John W. Yantis of Shelbyville as secretary.

WILLIAM S. CANTRELL, Chairman of the Board, was born in Benton, Ill., Feb. 6, 1851, and educated at the State University, Bloomington, Ind., taking the scientific course. He attended the Law School, at Shawneetown, conducted by Judge A. D. Duff, and was admitted to the bar in June, '74, and has practiced his profession ever since. He was states attorney of Franklin county for four years. He was married in March, '82 to Miss Jennie Burnett, of Shawneetown, and they have two children, a boy and a girl. He always has been very active in politics, and was a delegate to the National Democratic convention of '88, and took a lively interest in the campaign of '92. He was an enthusiastic friend of Gov. Altgeld before the democratic state convention, and devoted his talents and time to the election of the democratic state ticket, in the triumph of which he contributed not a little. He is a member of the grand lodge of Illinois, A. F. & A. M. and was on the law committee of the lodge--the committee on appeals and grievances--for ten years. He is also one of the supreme officers of the Knights of Honor. He was strongly endorsed for his present place, aud devotes his eutire time to the duties of the office.

CHAS. F. LAPE, was born in Zanesville, O., Nov. 22, 1842, and received a common school education while working on a farm up to the time he was 14 years old. Then he entered a boiler shop in Zanesville and learned the trade, remaining until '60, when he began braking for the Cincinnati, Wilmington & Zanesville railroad, now a branch of the Pennsylvania. In the spring of '61 he enlisted in Co. A, 3d O. Inf., but being under age his mother had his name stricken from the roll. Then he went on the L. & N. as brakeman, between Louisville and Nashville remaining until the spring of '62, when he accepted a place in the Ft. Wayne shops of the Wabash railroad. In '63 he worked for the I. & St. L., now the Big Four, at Litchfield, and in the spring of '64 he changed to the Illinois Central shops at Centralia. He was promoted to be assistant foreman and remained until '73, when he returned to the Ft.

CHAS. F. LAPE.

Wayne shops as foreman. In '82 he was made general foreman of the Andrews shops by J. B. Barnes. In '83 he removed to Danville, and assumed charge of the Tilton shops. Soon after he was made assistant master mechanic with headquarters at Mt. Carmel, and in '85 received his last promotion, being made master mechanic of the Springfield shops, which place he held until appointed to his present position. He married Miss Nancy Brown in Centralia, in '66, and has had four children, two of whom survive — a boy and girl. He is a Mason, an Elk, a director in two building and loan associations, and in the Franklin Life Insurance company. He is a Lutheran in religion, and never took a very active part in politics, being appointed to his present place on account of his knowledge of railroading — an appointment that met with general satisfaction.

THOS. GAHAN.

THOMAS GAHAN was born in Cook county, near Chicago, in 1849, and received a good common school education. In '66 he began life for himself as stock shipper for Nels Morris, and from '68 to '69 he represented Cragin & Hancock, packers in the Red River country. He was appointed patrolman of the Town of Lake in '70 when the force consisted of only three men; was promoted to be sergeant in '74; in '77 was made captain, which office he held until '84 when he was elected supervisor, treasurer and chief of police of the Town of Lake, three offices at that time consolidated. During the two years he held this office he handled $6,000,000 of the people's money. In '86 under the firm name of Gahan & Burns he engaged in the business of contracting for the building of sewers, laying water mains, etc. In '89 was elected alderman from the 29th ward, and started the fight to clear the Lake Front of the old exposition building and the B. & O. depot, in which he was successful. He was re-elected in '90, and resigned to accept his present office from Gov. Altgeld. When he entered the city council there was not a paved street in his ward, and when he left it, every street in his ward that was sewered had been paved or contracted to be paved. He is a member of the Iroquois Club, the Cook County Democracy, and the Marching Club, also of the I. O. F. and the A. O. U. W. He is a shrewd politician and contributed greatly to the success of the democratic ticket in the recent election.

JOHN W. YANTIS, Secretary of the Board, was born in Shelby county, May 13, 1855, and was educated at Westfield College and Bryant & Strattan's Business College, Chicago. He began life as clerk in a mercantile store in Shelbyville, and in '77 formed a partnership with his brother-in-law and bought a stock of dry goods, boots and shoes, which continued until '89, when he went into the real estate, loan and insurance business, which was his occupation, when he was appointed secretary of the board, March 1, '93. He was chairman of the county board for three years, and after his first race was elected without opposition. He was a member of the state board of equalization from '86 to '90. In '82 he married Miss Cordelia A. James, of Shelby county, and has four children,

J. W. YANTIS.

three girls and one boy. He attends the Christian church. He is a Mason, an Odd Fellow, an A. O. U. W. a Modern Woodman, and has been a representative to the grand lodge of Odd Fellows. Was on the committee on appeals for several years, and was chairman the last term. He is also on the committee on the state of the order in the Grand Encampment. Is chairman of the committee on appeals of the grand lodge, A. O. U. W., and is one of the trustees of the Odd Fellows Orphans' Home, at Lincoln. He has always been a working democrat in his section of the state.

JAS. H. PADDOCK.

JAMES H. PADDOCK, of this city, retiring secretary of the board, is one of the best known men connected with the politics of Illinois. For twenty-eight years past he has been in Springfield during the sessions of the general assembly. He was born in Lockport, Ill., May, 29, 1850, and received a good common school education. He was page in the senate in '65. In '67 he was assistant postmaster of the senate, and in '69, '71, '73 and '75 he was assistant secretary of the senate. In '77, '79 and '81 he was secretary of the senate. From '81 to '89 he was assistant secretary of state, and early in '89 he was appointed secretary of the railroad and warehouse commission, which position he filled until March 1, '93, when the change in administration permitted all the republican officials to retire. In '77 Mr. Paddock received the entire vote of the senate for secretary, when the farmers held the balance of power, and in '75 the democrats had the organization of the senate and they made him assistant secretary. He has never swerved from republicanism. Undoubtedly he has a wider acquaintance among the public men of Illinois than any other man in the state, and in every position he has occupied he has discharged his duties with an energy and faithfulness that commended him to his superiors.

In '73 he married Miss Mary L. Crawford, of Kankakee, and they have two children—a boy and girl.

THE PRINTER EXPERT.

Arthur L. Hereford, Printer Expert, was born in Secor, Woodford Co., Ill., April 1, 1858, and educated in the common school. He graduated from the Union College of Law, Chicago, in '78 and was admitted to the bar at Mt. Vernon in '79. He went west, and practiced for a short time at Concordia, Kan. In '80 he was nominated by the democratic state convention for attorney general of Kansas. He was prominent in Kansas politics for several years, and was vice president of the League of Democratic Clubs of that state in '80. But dollars were nearly as scarce as democrats in the Grasshopper state, and Mr. Hereford returned to Illinois, purchasing The El Paso Journal in Jan. '81, which he ran until Jan. '85, when he went to Chicago, and worked as a reporter on the staffs of The Chicago News, Tribune and other papers until '88. Then he returned to Woodford county and started The Metamora Herald, a democratic paper, which he ran until '91, when he sold out and purchased

A. L. HEREFORD.

The Mattoon Star, which he owns at this time. He was an enrolling and engrossing clerk of the house in the session of '91, and was appointed printer expert by Gov. Altgeld Jan. 19, '93. In Nov. '79, he married Miss Helen M. Jacquin, of Metamora, and has one son and one daughter.

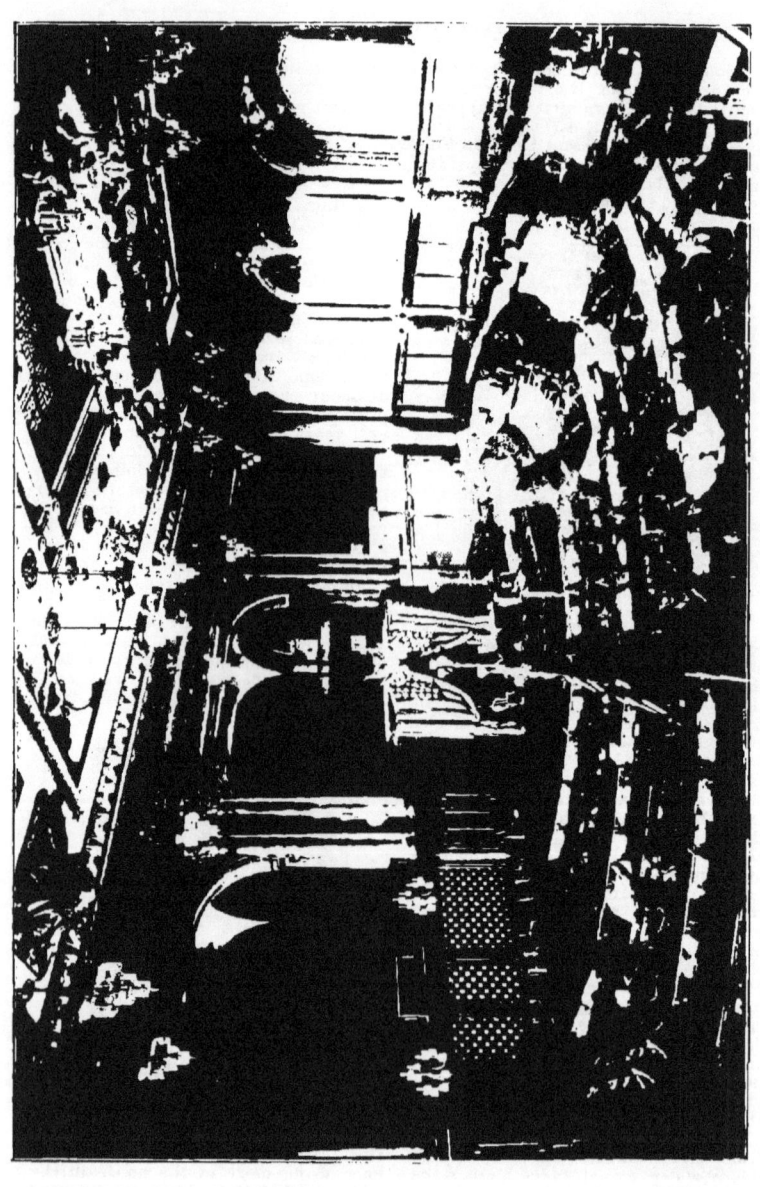

The Senate Chamber.

THE GENERAL ASSEMBLY.

For the first time in exactly thirty years a democratic general assembly convened in Springfield on the 4th day of January, 1893. It was more noteworthy from the fact that every department of the state government, and every office was filled or soon to be filled by democrats. The General Assembly for the State of Illinois operates under a constitution adopted by the people in 1870—the fourth instrument of the kind that has been submitted to the people, and the third that has been ratified and adopted—the constitution of 1862 having been rejected at the polls. The general assembly meets biennially at noon on the first Wednesday after the first Monday in January in odd-numbered years. It consists of a senate and a house of representatives numbering on joint ballot, 204. This is the Thirty-eighth General Assembly. In the biographies that follow the districts are not given, because it is expected that the present legislature will reapportion the state.

THE SENATE.

The Senate consists of 51 members, who are elected for four years, or two regular sessions. Senators from the odd numbered districts are elected at the same time as state treasurer and superintendent of public instruction—1886, 1890, 1894, etc. Senators from even-numbered districts are elected in presidential years—1888, 1892, 1896, etc. Senators receive $5 per diem during the session, $50 for stationery and 10 cents a mile for the actual distance from their homes to the state capital. The districts represented in the present general assembly were organized in 1881 by the republicans. The senate of 1893 consists of 29 democrats and 22 republicans.

THE OFFICERS.

Next to the President of the Senate the most influential officer is the Secretary. Indeed, he is often charged with passing or killing more bills than the senators. The present secretary, however, is above reproach, and never hastens or delays a roll call to permit the lobby to work, or stragglers sent for. This was almost a rule in the past.

Downing, Finis E., (dem.), Virginia; editor-lawyer. Secretary of the Senate. Born in Virginia, Aug. 24, 1846, and received a common school education. He left the farm when 16 and clerked in a dry goods store, afterwards going into the same line of trade for himself. In '69 he went to

SECRETARY DOWNING.

Butler, Mo., engaging in the grocery and dry goods business, in which he continued until '75. Then he returned to Cass county and was elected circuit clerk in '80, was re-elected in '84 and again in '88, his last term expiring last December. He was chosen secretary of the senate by the democratic caucus, and fills the place although the duties are entirely new, to the satisfaction of every senator. Is married. In Sept. '91 he bought The Virginia Enquirer, which is edited in his absence by his son, Harry F.

Davis, Robert H., Sergeant-at-Arms of the senate, lives in Carrollton, and was born in Mercer Co., Ky., about 55 years ago. In '32 his father moved to Greene Co., Ill., where he was a practicing physician, and very successful. Robert was educated in the district schools, and finished at Center College, Danville, Ky. He was salesman in a wholesale dry goods store in St. Louis for a time, and afterwards in a wholesale grocery and commission house. In '70 he went into the business of buying grain, selling flour and coal in Carrollton, and continued it until elected sergeant-at-arms. He was vice-president of the Mercantile Library, St. Louis, for two years and a director for four years; is a life member now; was a member of the board of education of Carrollton for twelve successive years, and was president of the board for six years. He was elected to the senate in '85 to succeed F. M. Bridges, deceased, and was returned

SERGEANT-AT-ARMS DAVIS.

to the house in '86 and '88. He was chosen seargeant-at-arms by acclamation in the democratic caucus.

Allen, Sylvester, (dem.), Oxvile. Scott Co.; farmer and merchant. Born in Jackson Co., O., Sept. 2, 1847, and received a common school education. He volunteered in the 7th Ohio cavalry and was rejected on account of his youth, but he was determined to go to the war, and was finally accepted as a teamster. After the war he settled in

SYLVESTER ALLEN.

Scott Co., Ill., on a farm near Oxville. Is married. He held the office of justice of the peace several times, and was postmaster of Oxville under President Cleveland. He was elected to the house in '88 and to the senate in '90, receiving 6,132 votes to 2,285 for B. B. Hamilton, rep., and 1,574 for R. T. Brock, bolting rep. In the house he took an active and honest interest in farmer legislation, and the record was continued in the senate in '91, when he was recognized as the champion of the interests of the agriculturists. Is a valuable member of the present senate. As a member of the faithful "101" in the last legislature Senator Allen was faithful and steadfast, regarding the voice of the people as a peremptory command.

Committees: Senatorial apportionment (chairman), visit charitable institutions (chairman), railroads, revenue, municipalities, charitable institutions, roads and bridges, military, building and loan associations, waterways and drainage, agriculture.

Anderson, Perry, (rep.), Alexis; lumber merchant. Born in Nasum Socken,

PERRY ANDERSON.

Christianstads Lan, Sweden, Oct. 5, 1853, and at the age of 19 determined to come to America. He did so, settling in Warren county and hiring out as a farm hand. His education in the English language was acquired in the high school of Alexis, and his commercial training at Davenport Business College. He rented a farm and followed agriculture for a time, but in '81 he engaged in the lumber business, and in that has been successful. In '92 he was instrumental in organizing the Alexis Stoneware Manufacturing Co., and is now serving as president of that enterprise. He has received many favors regardless of party; has been on the board of education many years, and is still a member; was on the board of village trustees and was president of the board, resigning when he was elected to the senate in '90. Is married. Is chairman of the present republican senate caucus.

Committees: Judicial department, warehouses, finance and claims, appropriations, municipalities, charitable institutions, penal and reformatory, world's fair, congressional apportionment, labor and manufactures.

Arnold, John W., (dem.), Lockport; merchant. Born on a farm in Washington county, New York, Feb. 14, 1852, and came to Illinois with his parents in 1855. Enlisted in the 4th Ill. Cav. under Col. Dickey, Sept. 16, '61; was discharged for disability in '62, re-enlisted in the Chicago Mercantile Battery, and was finally mustered out June 16, '65; was for 14 months a prisoner of war in Texas. After the war he engaged in business in Lockport. Was postmaster during the lat-

JOHN W. ARNOLD.

ter part of Cleveland's term. Is married. His popularity is evidenced from the votes he received for senator in '90, carrying Will county (the district) by 172, while his predecessor, a republican, was elected by a majority of 1,250, and in '92 Harrison carried it by 400. In the senate he is a hard worker and closely watches all measures.

Committees: Military (chairman), waterways and drainage (chairman), warehouses, revenue, municipalities, corporations, penal and reformatory, senatorial apportionment, world's fair, canals and rivers, agriculture, mines and mining, labor and manufactures.

Aspinwall, Homer F., (rep.), Freeport; farmer. Born in Stephenson county, Nov. 15, 1846, and was educated in the common schools, graduating from the Freeport high school. Then he clerked for two years in a wholesale notion store. Afterwards he began farming, and now owns 265

acres of land and is married. Has been on the board of supervisors for four years and held minor offices. He is a good specimen of a successful Illinois agriculturist, and takes great

HOMER F. ASPINWALL.

interest in matters that affect his constituents. Was elected in '92, receiving 8,748 votes to 7,905 for William Stewart, dem.

Committees: Elections, insurance, judicial department, agriculture, warehouses, revenue, penal and reformatory, state library, world's fair, senatorial apportionment.

Bacon, George E., (rep.), Paris; lawyer. Born on a farm near Madison, Ind., Feb. 4, 1851, and in '54 his parents moved to Coles Co., Ill., and in '76 he moved to Paris. His education was

GEORGE E. BACON.

finished at Northwestern University, Indianapolis, and the Union Law School, Chicago; was admitted in '79 at Ottawa. In a bar that possesses many great minds he has been as successful as any. Is married and has three children. Was elected to the senate in '86, and again in '90; was chairman of the republican caucus in '89. In '91 he refused to vote for any but a republican for U. S. senator—a position endorsed by the best element

CHARLES N. BARNES.

of his party. He is a man of fine physique, with a clear voice, and is one of the most effective and pleasing orators in the senate. His eulogy of Gen. Logan in '87 is referred to by those who heard it as an eloquent tribute, yet it was little better than his remarks on the death of Mr. Blaine and his old friend and colleague, Senator Matthews, during the present session. Few lawyers in Illinois, and probably none in the senate are the equals of Senator Bacon as a platform orator, a jury pleader or a lecturer. His services are in demand from all quarters of the state.

Committees: Judiciary, agriculture, education, elections, railroads, insurance, congressional apportionment, license and miscellany, labor and manufactures.

Barnes, Charles N., (dem.), Lacon; lawyer. Born in Marshall county, March 25, 1860, and was educated in the Washburn high school, at Iowa City College and the Chicago Law School; admitted to practice in '84. He has had a very successful run of cases ever since; was manager for the Springer Land Irrigating company in New Mexico for a time. He is married and owns 380 acres of land. He has represented his township three times on the county board, was states attorney of Marshall county for two years, and held various minor offices. He was elected to the senate in '92 by a vote of 8,039 to 6,325 for L. C. McMurtrie, rep. His colleagues in the senate have honored him with committee places far above those usually given a new member.

Committees: Canals and rivers (chairman), to visit penal and reformatory institutions (chairman), judiciary, judicial department, railroads, building and loan associations, world's fair, penal and reformatory, waterways and drainage, expenses of the general assembly, senatorial apportionment.

Bartling, Henry C., (dem.), Chicago; commission merchant and wholesale book dealer. Born in Springfield, Ill., July 4, 1867, and moved with his parents to Chicago in '70. He was educated in the Lutheran parochial schools. He was ledgerman at Marshall Field's for some time; has been in the commission business (grain and produce) for four years, and at the same time handles church and school books—books of the Lutheran church and the public schools. He is not married. He was elected supervisor for the North Town in '91, being second on the ticket, although the district is safely republican. He was a delegate to the last state convention and member of the committee on resolutions. He is very popular in his own district; elected in '92 by a vote of 20,801 to 17,181 for J. H. Muhlke, rep. The district was overwhelmingly republican

HENRY C. BARTLING.

in '88. Senator Bartling is one of the youngest members of the legislature, and is honored with good committees.

Committees: License and miscellany (chairman), municipalities, public buildings, education, fees and salaries, printing, elections, building and loan associations, world's fair, waterways and drainage, congressional apportionment, canals and rivers.

Bass, George, (rep.), Chicago; lawyer. Born in Williamstown, Vt., Dec. 10, 1847, and moved to Chicago in '60. He was educated in the public schools and graduated at Harvard in '71. Holds a high place as a member of the Chicago bar, served as South Town collector in '90; was a republican pres-

GEORGE BASS.

idential elector in '80, and was elected to the senate in the fall of '90 by a vote of 4,464 to 4,225 for Lawrence P. Boyle, dem. Is not married. He takes little interest in the lower strata of politics, and yet is regarded by all elements as a safe leader in a campaign.

Committees: Judiciary, warehouses, senatorial apportionment, finance and claims, municipalities, insurance, building and loan associations, corporations, world's fair, congressional apportionment, license and miscellany.

Berry, Orville F., (rep.), Carthage; lawyer. Born in McDonough county, Feb. 16, 1852, and was early left an orphan. He received a common school education, and at 16 began life's battle for himself, and after working as a farm hand and running a farm, he removed to Carthage, where he read law; admitted to the bar in '77. In '79 formed a partnership with his brother M. P., and they have had a very successful practice ever since. In '83 he was elected mayor of Carthage and was twice re-elected without opposition. He was secretary of the Hancock county agricultural board for four years, and acted as superintendent one year. He has been grand master workman of the A. O. U. W. of Illinois, and has been supreme representative from Illinois at several sessions of the supreme lodge. From the supreme lodge he has been delegate to fraternal congresses. He is also a Modern Woodman and a Royal Arch Mason. Is married. Was elected to the senate in '88, and again in '92, running ahead of his ticket both times; in '92 he received 7,260 votes to 7,016 for Edward L. Wolf, dem. In the legislature of '91 he strongly advocated compulsory education and the retention of the compulsory teaching of English in all the schools of the state, and a vindictive fight was made on him at the polls last year in consequence.

Committees: Judiciary, judicial department, railroads, corporations, charitable institutions, education, elections, senatorial apportionment, world's fair, canals and rivers.

Bogardus, Charles, (rep.) Paxton; farmer and stock raiser. Born in Cayuga Co., N. Y., March 28, 1841, and left an orphan at 6 years old. He had to carve out his own future, succeeding as the record shows. He was educated in the common schools and began working in a store at 12 years of age. In '62 he enlisted in the 151st N. Y. Inf.; was elected first lieutenant, and came out of the service as a lieutenant-colonel, brevetted colonel "for gallant and meritorious services before Petersburg." He came to Illinois in '72 and has since resided in Ford county, dealing in lands and operat-

ORVILLE F. BERRY.

ing many splendid farms and raising fine stock. Is married. He was a member of Gov. Oglesby's and subsequently Gov. Fifer's military staff, with the rank of colonel. He declined to give the number of acres of land he owns, but his Illinois holdings are not far from 5,000 acres, as learned from other sources. Was elected to the house in '84 and '86, and to the senate in '88 and '92. He is a man of great force of character, indomitable energy and quick business instinct, and no

CHARLES BOGARDUS.

man in the general assembly is more popular or influential. He was chairman of the republican caucus in '87, and chairman of the committee to make up the republican membership of the senate committees in '89 and '93.

Committees: Revenue, penal and reformatory, military, roads and bridges, senatorial apportionment, building and loan associations, world's fair, congressional apportionment, agriculture.

Brands, Albert L., (dem.), Prairie du Rocher; physician. Born on

ALBERT L. BRANDS.

a farm in St. Genevieve Co., Mo., April 26, 1856. He received a common school education, followed by a term at DeSoto academy, Missouri. His medical education was obtained at the Missouri Medical college in St. Louis, graduating in '80, and moved the same year to Ivy Landing, Monroe, Co., Ill., and thence to his present home in Sept. '81. Is married. He has never held office before, and was elected in '92 to the state senate over James Boston, rep., by a majority of 850. He is consistent in his opposition to any legislation that will be likely to foster trusts or monopolies, and is a farmer champion.

Committees: Expenses of the general assembly (chairman), library, building and loan associations, canals and rivers, mines and mining, county and township organization, senatorial apportionment, roads and bridges, charitable institutions, appropriations, education, military, penal and reformatory.

Caldwell, Ben F., (dem.), Chatham; farmer and banker. Born near Car-

BEN. F. CALDWELL.

rollton, Ill., Aug. 2, 1848, moving with his father to Sangamon county in '53. Most of his youth was spent on a farm; was educated in the Chatham schools. After his marriage he made a tour of Europe. He is a Past Master in Masonry, and has taken the 32d degree; is an Elk and a Past Noble Grand in the Odd Fellows. He was a member of the house in '83 and '85, and accomplished more for his constituents than any representative the capitol district ever had in the legislature. He has served two terms as member and one as chairman of the county board of supervisors. He is one of the wealthiest members of the legislature and is in politics for recreation and to do good. He is a very industrious and influential member. His farming interests are very large. Is president of the Farmers' National bank of this city, of the Bank of Virden, and the Bank of Chatham. During the session of '91 he introduced and successfully advocated the bill reducing the rate of interest from 8 to 7 per cent., notwithstanding he is a banker and capitalist. His popularity is attested by the fact

JAMES R. CAMPBELL.

that he ran away ahead of his ticket in '90, having been elected senator over P. H. Donnelly, rep. by 7,106 to 5,340—the district being democratic by about 900.

Committees: Banks and banking (chairman), railroads, finance and claims, revenue, insurance, corporations, public buildings, printing, roads and bridges, senatorial apportionment, state library, agriculture, mines and mining.

Campbell, James R., (dem.), McLeansboro; editor-lawyer. Born in Crook township, Hamilton Co., May 4, 1853. His ancestors emigrated from County Armagh, Ireland, and Crook township was named after his greatgrandfather. He was reared on a farm, educated at Notre Dame, and taught school after completing his education. In the meantime he read law and was admitted to the bar in '77. In '78 he purchased The McLeansboro Times, the only democratic paper in the county, and has since edited it, besides being an extensive breeder of Percheron horses and a large land owner. He was elected to the house in '84 and '86, and advanced to the senate by a constituency that appreciated his work, in '88, and again in '92. In '85 he rendered valuable assistance to Speaker Haines in selecting the house committees. In the senate in '91 he introduced and secured the passage of a bill reducing one-third the maximum price on public printing, and making it impossible for a combination to control the bidding on state contracts. He has been energetic this year in an endeavor to carry out the pledges of the democratic platform in regard to covering the interest on state monies into the treasury.

Committees: Printing (chairman), federal relations (chairman), judiciary, railroads, revenue, insurance, charitable institutions, education, senatorial apportionment, agriculture, license and miscellany, county and township organization.

Chapman, Pleasant T., (rep.), Vienna; lawyer and banker, was born in Johnson county on a farm Oct. 8, 1854, where he lived until he was 19 years old. He graduated from McKendree college in '76, and was admitted to the bar at Mt. Vernon in '78. In '77 he was elected superintendent of Johnson county's schools, and reappointed for a short term in '81; next year was chosen county judge, and again in '86, his term expiring Dec. 1, '90. In Nov. '90, he was elected to the senate, receiving 6,622 votes to 6,048 for C. M. Farris, dem. He is married and is largely interested in real estate and farms, besides being president of the First National bank of Vienna. He taught school during vacations while attending college and for two years afterwards, and has been engaged in

PLEAS T. CHAPMAN.

banking, the law, mercantile business and farming for the past twelve years in Johnson county, meantime mixing in politics to some extent as the above proves.

Committees: Judiciary, railroads, revenue, insurance, banks and banking, public buildings, roads and bridges, federal relations, senatorial apportionment.

Coon, Reuben W., (rep.), Waukegan; editor and publisher. Born May 31, 1842 at Frankfort, Clinton Co., Ind. In '48 his father, who was a minister, moved to Peoria Co., Ill., where he remained until '55, when he moved to Alton, and here Senator Coon received his education at Shurtleff College. He lived in Pana from '61 to '70, and in '69 was assistant secretary of the state senate. While in Pana he practiced law, and had one-half interest in The Gazette. In '70 he moved to Belvidere and bought The Belvidere Northwestern, which he owned and made very influential until '85 when he sold it and bought The Waukegan Gazette, one of the best country papers in the state, and one of the most powerful republican organs in Northern Illinois. He was states attorney of Boone county from '80 to '84, and was elected to the in '90. In the session of '91 he introduced a bill and was largely instrumental in securing its enactment repealing "the Merritt Conspiracy Act." He was chosen president pro tem of the

JOHN W. COPPINGER.

senate this year by the unanimous voice of the democratic caucus, and while Lieut. Gov. Gill was acting governor, filled the chair in the senate with dignity and satisfaction.

Committees: Mines and mining (chairman), rules, judicial department, railroads, municipalities, military, elections, congressional apportionment, canals and rivers, labor and manufactures.

Craig, Isaac B., (dem.), Mattoon; lawyer. Born in Coles county April 28, 1857. He was educated in the pub-

REUBEN W. COON.

senate in '92 by a vote of 8,143 to 4,764 for Charles N. Smith, dem. He has always been a republican and active in all campaigns.

Committees: Judiciary, appropriations, municipalities, banks and banking, printing, senatorial apportionment, building and loan associations, worlds fair, revenue, enrolled and engrossed bills, joint committee on enrolled and engrossed bills.

Coppinger, John W., (dem.), Alton; stone contractor. Born in Alton Jan. 12, 1852, and was educated in the public schools of Alton, St. Mary's College, Perryville, Mo., and at Notre Dame. He read law and was admitted to the bar in '72. He has been mayor of Alton. Is married. He is popular with his colleagues and has a very extensive and valuable acquaintance throughout the state. He was elected to the house in '86, and to the senate

ISAAC B. CRAIG.

lic schools and at Ann Arbor. He has been a very successful practitioner at Mattoon for twelve years. He has always taken great interest in politics, and has filled various local offices. He was elected to the house in '88, and again in '90, and promoted to the senate in '92, running ahead of his ticket, the district being republican on the head of the ticket. Is married. Was chairman of the caucus, and appointed the steering committee of democrats that managed the Palmer contest for United States senator in '91. He is a member of the same committee in the senate this year, and is one of the democratic leaders on the floor. Mr. Craig is an earnest and effective orator, and one of the best members of the senate.

Committees: Corporations (chairman), judiciary, judicial department, revenue, appropriations, insurance, senatorial apportionment, building and loan associations, state library-arts and sciences, county and township organization.

Crawford, William F., (rep.), Taylor Ridge, Rock Island Co.; farmer. Born in Clark Co., Ind., July 7, 1835, and moved to Rock Island county with his parents in '42. His father died when he was 8 years old, and he went out to work on a farm, receiving only $6 a month. He continued this until he was 18, when he was able to make a full hand. During this time he attended the district schools as best he could. He is married and is a successful farmer, owning 320 acres of splendid land which he accumulated by his

WILLIAM F. CRAWFORD.

own industry. He has held various local offices of minor importance, and was elected to the house in '86 and '88, and promoted to the senate in '90, receiving 7,720 votes to 6,309 for R. H. Hinman, dem. He enlisted in the army in Aug. '61 in the 9th Ill. Cav., and served over three years. He participated in the battle of Tupelo and saw a great deal of hard service. He is a strong representative of the farmers' interests in the legislature.

Committees: Expenses of the general assembly, corporations, charitable institutions, public buildings, roads and bridges, federal relations, canals and rivers, agriculture, mines and mining, county and township organization.

HENRY M. DUNLAP.

Dunlap, Henry M., (rep.), Savoy; farmer and fruit grower, was born in Cook county, Nov. 14, 1853, and four years later his parents moved to Savoy, where he has lived ever since. He was educated in the University of Illinois at Urbana, graduating in the class of '75 in the scientific course. Is married and owns 320 acres of land, 200 of which are in bearing apple orchards. Represented for six years Champaign township on the county board, has been president of the State Horticultural society, and is a K. P. in good standing. He takes great interest in all matters pertaining to agriculture and horticulture.

Committees: Appropriations, revenue, agriculture, roads and bridges, county and township organization, banks and banking, waterways and drainage, penal and reformatory, fees and salaries, building and loan associations.

Evans, Henry H., (rep.), Aurora; real estate capitalist. The oldest member of the legislature in consecutive service. Born in Toronto, Canada, March 9, 1836, and moved to Aurora in '41. Mr. Evans' father was for ten years foreman of the car building shops of the Burlington system. Is married. Was elected to the house in '76 and to the senate in '80, '84, '88, '92, the last time by a vote of 10,278 to 7,929 for Chester D. Bartlett, dem. Was the republican nominee for president pro tem, is by virtue of it the leader of his party, and as such was conceded a chairmanship with clerk and room where his party colleagues can retire for consultation. Is financially interested in real estate and corporate property to a large extent. He is one of the most influential members, and is regarded as a man of ability. Opposed the election of Streeter to the U. S. senate in '91 by the republicans and refused to vote for him, although willing to abide by caucus action if a straight-out republican was selected. His constituents endorsed his position by returning him to the senate in '92 by an increased majority.

Committees: state library-arts and sciences (chairman), railroads, revenue, insurance, corporations, banks and banking, printing, military, building and loan associations, agriculture, license and miscellany.

hotbed of the F. M. B. A. movement in that year, and a tremendous effort was made to defeat him. He is deservedly popular and is one of the leaders in the senate. His tastes run in the way of

WILLIAM M. FARMER.

judicial honors rather than political office.

Committees: Judiciary (chairman), judicial department, expenses of general assembly, banks and banking, building and loan associations, state library, agriculture, congressional apportionment, world's fair.

Ferguson, Virgil S., (rep.), Sterling; lawyer. Born in Lawrence Co., Ind., Sept. 18, 1844. Five years later his father, who was a descendent of one of five brothers who emigrated from Scotland before the revolutionary war,

HENRY H. EVANS.

Farmer, William M., (dem.), Vandalia; lawyer. Born in Fayette county, June 5, 1853; lived on a farm and attended district school until he was 18 years old, when he entered McKendree college. Then he taught school and began reading law in the office of Henry & Fouke in Vandalia. In '75 he entered the Union College of Law in Chicago in the junior class and graduated next year. He was immediately admitted to the bar and began active work as a lawyer in Vandalia, where he has met with almost phenomenal success. For ten years he has been senior member of the firm Farmer & Brown. In '80 was elected states attorney, and in '88 to the house, his constituents promoting him to the senate in '90, although his district was the

VIRGIL S. FERGUSON.

located in Whiteside county, and engaged in farming on a large scale. Senator Ferguson attended the public schools and graduated from the law department of the University of Chicago in '68; was admitted to the bar the same year, and has since been in successful practice in Sterling. Is married. He is a strong advocate of compulsory education, and just as strongly in favor of the teaching of English in all the schools. He served on the board of supervisors for ten years or more; is now and has been for fifteen years on the board of education; was elected to the senate in '90 by a vote of 5,711 to 4,449 for J. M. Eaton, dem. He never missed a roll call for U. S. senator in '91, although so ill part of the time that his life was despaired of by his friends and physicians. He is a good representative, faithful and prompt in his attendance.

Committees: Judiciary, judicial department, appropriations, penal and reformatory, education, world's fair, congressional apportionment, canals and rivers, mines and mining.

Ford, Thomas E., (dem.), Carlyle; lawyer. Born on a farm in Clinton county, May 24, 1848. His father was a member of the assembly of '63—a democrat, of course. From a newspaper in his district it is learned that Senator Ford's history is that of one of the most remarkable men in Illinois, illustrating the wonderful qualities of pioneer manhood. Born and reared on a farm, with most meager opportunities for learning, he somehow con-

THOMAS E. FORD.

trived to acquire a fair education. As a youth he was a leader in local debating societies, which led to an extensive practice before justices of the peace of the vicinity, and afterwards to a large law practice; admitted to the bar in '79. He has been active in politics since '74, and has held various local offices. Is married. Was elected to the senate in '92 over J. H. Fricke, rep., by a vote of 5,711 to 4,877.

Committees: Education (chairman), judiciary, judicial department, railroads, finance and claims, revenue, public buildings, fees and salaries, printing, military, building and loan associations, world's fair, congressional apportionment, agriculture.

REED GREEN.

Green, Reed, (dem.), Cairo; lawyer. Born in Mt. Vernon, Ill., Sept. 22, 1865, and educated in the Southern Illinois Normal University. On completing his education he taught school for two years in Cairo. He attended the Wesleyan Law School at Bloomington, graduating in '84, was admitted to the bar the same year, and has practiced since he was 21 years old, meeting with decided success. He is at present a member of the law firm of Green & Gilbert, of Cairo, one of the oldest and most famous in all "Egypt." He was elected to the house in '88, returned in '90, and advanced to the senate with no effort on his own part to secure the nomination in '92, receiving 7,205 votes to 6,465 for J. E. N. Edwards, rep. He was chairman of the house committee on elections in '91, and practically drafted the present Australian election law. He is one of the most eloquent and forcible speakers in the legislature, and a leader on the floor. Is not married. Senator Green made an exceptionally brilliant record while in the house in '89-'91.

Committees: Roads, highways and bridges (chairman); visit educational institutions (chairman), judiciary, railroads, municipalities, insurance, education, elections, building and loan associations, congressional apportionment, labor, license, county and township organization.

Hamer, Thomas, (rep.), Vermont; retired merchant. The oldest member of the general assembly. Was born in Union Co., Penn., June 1, 1818, and in '46 he moved to Illinois and established himself in business in Vermont. Received a common school education. Is married. In August, '62, he assisted in recruiting the 84th Illinois regiment, and was made lieutenant-colonel. He was wounded in the left breast and shoulder at Stone River, but the wounds healing over, he continued in active service until they broke out and incapacitated him for further service. He returned home and resumed business until '78, when he retired. He was offered the place of post commander at Franklin, Tenn., but he declined, preferring home to anything but service in the field. He was elected to the house in '86 and to the senate

THOMAS HAMER.

in '88 and '92, the last time receiving 10,704 votes to 8,298 for Levi K. Byers, dem. He is highly respected by his colleagues.

Committees: Charitable institutions, public buildings and grounds, military, visit charitable institutions, waterways and drainage, congressional apportionment, canals and rivers, mines and mining, labor and manufactures.

Higbee, Harry, (dem.), Pittsfield; lawyer. Born in Pittsfield Dec. 13, 1854, the son of the late Judge Chauncey L. Higbee. Finished his education at Yale, entering in '71 and graduating in '75, and completed his law studies at the Columbia Law School, New York, and the Union College of Law, Chicago, from which he graduated in '78. He then traveled in Europe for nine months accompanied by Congressman Scott Wike, and on returning formed a law partnership with Mr. Wike, which still exists. Was married in '79, and lost his wife in '81. Has held various local offices, and was elected to the senate in '88 and again

HARRY HIGBEE.

in '92, running ahead of his ticket each time. He is largely interested in farm lands. Is chairman of the democratic senate caucus, and the leader of his party on the floor. Is strong in debate, an indefatigable worker, a good parliamentarian and very popular with political friend and foe.

Committees: Appropriations (chairman), judiciary, banks and banking, fees and salaries, state library, world's fair, congressional apportionment, canals and rivers, agriculture.

VINTON E. HOWELL.

Howell, Vinton E., (rep.), Bloomington; farmer, was born in Licking Co., O., Nov. 30, 1840, and moved to McLean county in '52. He was educated in the common schools, with one term in the Normal college. When the war broke out he enlisted in Co. C, 33d Ill. Inf., and served over three years. After the war he engaged in farming and stock raising, in which he has been very successful. He was elected sheriff of McLean county in '86 for four years without opposition. He has been a member of the county board for five years, is married and owns considerable land. He was elected to the senate in '92 over his old neighbor, Hon. Simeon H. West, dem., by a vote of 7,391 to 6,478. Senator Howell is a hard worker in the senate, and informs himself of the merits of every bill that comes up.

Committees: Revenue, municipalities, fees and salaries, state institutions, roads and bridges, building and loan associations, visit penal and reformatory institutions.

Humphrey, John, (rep.), Orland; lawyer. Born in the county of Norfolk, England, June 20, 1838, and was brought to this country by his parents a lad of ten years. The family settled in Cook county, where he received a common school education. He read law in the office of Hon. James P. Root, and was admitted to the bar in '72. He has lived in Orland for many years, and practices his profession with an office in Chicago. Is married and owns 280 acres of land in Cook county. He has been treasurer of Orland for twenty years and supervisor

JOHN HUMPHREY.

for twenty-four years. He was once a bailiff under Sheriff Bradley. He was elected to the house in '70, also in '80, and again in '84, and was advanced to the senate in '86, and returned in '90 in the face of a determined opposition, by a vote of 8,772 to 7,939 for Louis Wagner, dem. Senator Humphrey's long service has not been without recognition, for he is on the most desirable committees. He is one of the most influential members.

Committees: Judiciary, judicial department, railroads, warehouses, municipalities, senatorial apportionment, waterways and drainage, congressional apportionment, license and miscellany.

DANIEL D. HUNT.

Hunt, Daniel D., (rep.), DeKalb; farmer. Born Sept. 19, 1835, in Wyoming Co., N. Y., and came to DeKalb county in '57. For the last twenty years he has been a successful farmer and has held various local offices, such as supervisor, school trustee, etc. He was educated in the public schools. Is married. Was elected to the house in '86 and '88, and to the senate in '90. In the last senate he was chairman of the committees on agriculture, horticulture and farm drainage and live stock and dairying. He has at all times served his state and district creditably, and has introduced and secured the passage of numerous important measures. Was the champion of the dairy interest in both house and senate.

Committees: Judicial department, insurance, corporations, fees and salaries, senatorial apportionment, building and loan associations, world's fair, mines and mining, labor and manufactures, county and township organization.

Hunter, David, (rep.), Rockford; farmer. Was born in Wyoming Co., N. Y., Jan. 15, 1836, and came to Illinois with his parents in '44. His father settled on a farm six miles from Rockford, which Mr. Hunter still occupies. He was for three years a private in Co. C, 15th Ill. Inf., enlisting May 24, '61. He was educated in the common schools of pioneer Illinois; is married, and owns 160 acres of Winnebago county land. He has held various minor offices, and has been continuously a member of the Illinois legislature since '84, when he was elected to the house, and was returned in '86, '88, '90, and in '92 he was advanced to the senate. Senator Evans and Speaker Crafts are the only two members who have served longer continuously, while Senators Campbell, Bogardus and Mahoney began in the house the same session as himself. He is one of the best members of the legislature, and is always present during sessions.

Committees: Revenue, penal and reformatory, municipalities, military, elections, agriculture, county and township organization, finance and claims.

DAVID HUNTER.

Johnson, C. Porter, (dem.), Chicago; lawyer. Born in Vermilion Co., Ill., Aug. 15, 1866. His path was not strewn with roses in early life, and every step on the ladder has been earned by hard work and close application. His ability as a lawyer and his usefulness as a legislator were not advertised in advance of his time. This is his first public office, and he is already recognized as one of the most fluent public speakers and the equal in debate of any senator. He was educated at Lee's Academy in Coles county, and was admitted to the bar in '87, opening an office in Chicago the same year, and has a large and profitable practice. He was town attorney for the Town of Lake in '90, and in '92 was tendered the nomination for congress, but declined, and was elected senator from the Second district, which gave an overwhelming republican majority for Harrison in '88, receiving 28,326 votes to 27,367 for Perry A. Hull, rep.

Committees: Enrolled and engrossed bills (chairman), elections (chairman), joint com-

C. PORTER JOHNSON.

mittee on enrolled and engrossed bills (chairman), judiciary, railroads, revenue, municipalities, banks and banking, penal and reformatory, visit charitable institutions, world's fair, congressional apportionment, agriculture

Knopf, Philip, (rep.), Chicago; real estate and loans. Born at Long Grove, Lake Co., Ill., Nov. 18, 1847. and moved to Chicago in '66. He was educated in the public schools and at Bryant & Stratton's Business College, where he spent one year. Is married.

PHILIP KNOPF.

In the spring of '65 he enlisted in Co. I, 147th Ill. Inf., when not quite 16 years old. He was elected to the senate in '86 and re-elected in '90 by a vote of 7,209 to 5,782 for Thomas J. Diven, dem. He was chief deputy coroner of Cook county for eight years under Henry L. Hertz. Has taken prominent part in all legislation, par-

ARTHUR A. LEEPER.

ticularly as affecting Cook county; he is always in attendance.

Committees: Judicial department, education, railroads, municipalities, fees and salaries, military, federal relations, waterways and drainage, congressional apportionment, license and miscellany.

Leeper, Arthur A., (dem.), Virginia; lawyer. Born on a farm near Chandlerville, Cass county, Aug. 21, 1855. He was educated in the common schools and at Eureka College, and graduated from the law department of the State

GEORGE R. LETOURNEAU.

University at Iowa City in '75. Is married. Senator Leeper was states attorney of Cass county from '76 to '80, and was elected state senator in

'88 for four years, and was re-elected in '92 by a vote of 7,998 to 5,979 for W. M. Grimwood, rep. The Senator is a man of firmness and recognized ability as a lawyer and parliamentary tactician. He stands high with his colleagues in the senate, and was chosen chairman of the committee on railroads this session but declined.

Committees: Railroads, judiciary, judicial department, corporations, insurance, rules, roads and bridges, canals and rivers, senatorial apportionment.

Letourneau, George R., (rep.), Kankakee; lumber and coal dealer, retired. Born in St. Thomas, Canada, Feb. 28, 1833, and in '47 came alone to Illinois. After remaining a year in Chicago, he caught the gold fever and struck across the plains for California. In '52 he returned and settled at Bourbonnais Grove, then in Will county, now in

JOSEPH P. MAHONEY.

Kankakee, where he remained until '83, when he moved to Kankakee. He received a good common school education. He was elected circuit clerk in '72, sheriff in '82, and county treasurer in '86, and in '92 was elected senator, receiving 7,387 votes to 6,672 for A. L. Granger, dem. Is married but lost his wife six years ago. He has had twelve children and all are living.

Committees: Railroads, appropriations, public buildings, canals and rivers, license and miscellany, mines and mining, labor and manufactures, printing, county and township organization.

Mahoney, Joseph P., (dem.), Chicago; lawyer. Born in Oswego, N. Y., Nov. 1, 1863, and moved to Chicago with his parents in '66. He was educated in the public schools and graduated at the West Side high school. Then he read law in the office of Hon. John N. Jewett, and was admitted to the bar in '84, and elected the same year to the house, being 21 years of age the Saturday preceding election day. He was re-elected to the house in '86 and '88, and advanced to the senate in '90 by a vote of 7,946 to 3,707 for James Monahan, rep. He is one of the oldest members of the legislature in continuous service. Is not married. Senator Mahoney is one of the readiest debaters and best parliamentarians in the state; quick in retort and apt in repartee. He was appointed to the board of education in Chicago last year by Mayor Washburn, but resigned. He has an extensive law practice and is very successful in his profession.

Committees: Penal and reformatory (chairman), judiciary, warehouses, appropriations, municipalities, insurance, corporations, banks and banking, education, elections, senatorial apportionment, world's fair, waterways and drainage, license and miscellany.

Manecke, Harmon, (dem.), Oakley, Macon Co.; farmer. Born in Hancock Co., O., Dec. 16, 1850, and at 11 years of age was left an orphan. He worked on a farm and attended district school and the high school at Fostoria several terms. In '68 he moved to Macon county and worked as a farm hand until '72, when he commenced farming for himself. Was elected town clerk of Oakley in '74 and served three terms and has represented his township on

HARMON MANECKE.

the board of supervisors for eleven terms. Is married. Was elected to the senate in '90 by a majority of over 1,000, although the district was strongly republican, receiving 6,927 votes to 5,902 for James Milliken, rep. In '72 he became a democrat, when war taxes and protective tariffs were first discussed since the war. There is no more conscientious nor industrious member of the legislature.

Committees: Agriculture (chairman), judicial department, appropriations, municipalities, charitable institutions, railroads, roads and bridges, congressional apportionment, mines and mining, county and township organization.

WILLIAM A. MUSSETT.

Mussett, William A., (rep.), Grayville; teacher. Born in Grayville Jan. 2, 1865, and educated at the Danville (Ind.) Normal and the Indiana University at Bloomington, graduating as the president of the class of '89, and was second in the oratorical contest of that year. Was superintendent of the Grayville schools from '89 to '92, and brought them up to a high point of efficiency. Is not married. He has made a particularly good impression on the senators, and will ultimately make the law his profession. Was elected to the senate in '92, receiving 6,964 votes to 6,198 for the old veteran politician and democratic war horse, James C. Allen—a decided compliment to Mr. Mussett's popularity and ability.

Committees: Judicial department, warehouses, expenses of general assembly, corporations, education, elections, senatorial apportionment, to visit educational institutions, state library.

Niehaus, John M., (dem.), Peoria; lawyer, was born in Warendorf, Westphalia, Feb. 15, 1855. The Senator's father, who was a hardware merchant in the old country, emigrated to America the same year and the family followed a year later, stopping first at Pittsburg for a year and then removing to Peoria, where the family has lived ever since. John M. was educated principally in private German schools, having special instruction in Latin and the classics; he also spent a term in a business college, graduating in '71. Read law with

JOHN M. NIEHAUS.

O'Brien & Harmon, was admitted to the bar in '74, and began practice in '77. Was elected to the house in '80 and was chosen state's attorney of Peoria county in '83 to fill an unexpired term, being re-elected in '84 and again in '88; elected senator in '92.

Committees: Congressional apportionment (chairman), judiciary, warehouses, revenue, municipalities, penal and reformatory, fees and salaries, building and loan associations, world's fair, waterways and drainage, canals and rivers, agriculture.

EDWARD T. NOONAN.

Noonan, Edward T., (dem.), Chicago. Born in Macomb, Ill., October 23, 1861. His father, an officer under Sherman, was killed in the battle of Atlanta. He moved to Chicago with his mother in '68, and now resides at 398 Washington boulevard. Received the degree of L. L. B. from the University of Michigan, and read law with Judge Van H. Higgins, and Hon. C. C. Bonney. Was admitted to the bar in '82, and is now engaged in the practice of real estate and corporation law. Was appointed aid-de-camp, with rank as colonel, on the staff of Governor Altgeld. Is president of the Building Society Secretaries' Club, and is a member of the Iroquois, Ashland, White Chapel and Sheridan clubs of Chicago, and is not married. Was the first democratic senator ever elected from his district and was one of the noble "101".

Senator Noonan is a member of several important committees.

ANDREW J. O'CONOR.

O'Conor, Andrew J., (dem.), LaSalle; lawyer. Born in LaSalle, July 19, 1852, and received his education in the schools of that city and at Niagara College. Taught school two years and read law at the same time; was admitted to practice in '76. He formed a law partnership with Hon. James W. Duncan, whose sister he married the same year. The partnership continued until '86, when Mr. Duncan moved to Chicago. Mr. O'Conor has the faculty of attracting to him friends who are with him to the death. Has held minor offices at home, mayor, city attorney, school treasurer, etc., and when he entered the senate in '91 he assumed a commanding position as democratic leader. Senator O'Conor possesses the confidence of Governor Altgeld probably more than any other man outside the governor's family, and had a great deal to do with shaping the work of the last democratic state convention, and he could have had the nomination for attorney general in '92 without asking for it.

Committees: World's columbian exposition (chairman), labor and manufactures (chairman), judiciary, judicial department, appropriations, penal and reformatory, education, federal relations, elections, congressional apportionment, canals and rivers, mines and mining.

O'Malley, John F., (dem.). Chicago: clerk. Born in Chicago, April 12, 1860. Educated in Chicago's public schools. Began earning a living for himself in the coal yards of the north side, and afterwards entered into partnership in the sale of coal with Mr. Mullins. Is not married. Was elected supervisor for the North Town in '84, and was re-elected in '85. For several years he was clerk in the office of North Town Assessor Samuel B. Chase. He is a staunch democrat and never wavered in his fidelity to Gen. Palmer during the senatorial fight of '91. Was elected state senator in '90 over Michael F. Garrity, rep. by a vote of 5,218 to 3,035. Senator O'Malley is one of the best workers in the democratic party in Cook county, and is generally a winner

Committees: Warehouses (chairman), judicial department, expenses of the general assembly, corporations, charitable institutions, penal and reformatory, public buildings, federal relations, senatorial apportionment, world's fair, license and miscellany, labor and manufactures.

JOHN F. O'MALLEY.

Paisley, George W., (dem.), Hillsboro; farmer, coal operator and lawyer, was born in Montgomery county, March 1, 1838, and was educated in the common schools and at Hillsboro Academy. Entered the army in '62 and served three years in Co. I. 122d Ill. Inf., and on his return from the war was elected county surveyor. Then he studied law and was admitted in '70, and practiced for about six years, when he founded The Montgomery News, a democratic newspaper of wide influence. Was chosen

GEORGE W. PAISLEY.

master in chancery and served from '68 to '79. Was elected to the house in '80, and in '85 was appointed one of three inspectors of surveyors of the general and district land offices by President Cleveland, and resigned in May '89, after opening one of the land offices in Oklahoma. Is married. Is one of the best posted men in Illinois on revenue and taxation questions. Is a careful and industrious member, of pronounced ability, and was elected to the senate by a vote of 7,331 to 5,842 for W. W. Weeden, rep.

Committees: Rules (chairman), revenue (chairman), judiciary, appropriations, corporations, printing, visit educational institutions, congressional apportionment, mines and mining.

Reavill, Andrew J., (dem.), Flat Rock, Crawford Co.; farmer and stockman. Born Dec. 24, 1834, on the farm he now owns, one mile and one-half from Flat Rock. His father located there in '17, and nobody will dispute Senator Reavill's claim as a pioneer of the state. Senator Reavill's education was limited to the rudiments of learning, taught in the district schools of that primitive time. Is married. Was a member of the house in '77 and '79, and chosen to represent his district in the senate in '86 and again in '90. The senator has been a life-long democrat, and enjoys the confidence of his constituents. He has accumulated a competency by close application, untiring industry and shrewdness. Was one of the most important figures and did not a little to insure the election of Gen.

ANDREW J. REAVILL.

Palmer to the senate in '91. He is a quiet, unostentatious, yet a very shrewd member.

Committees: County and township organization (chairman), railroads, warehouses, finance and claims, expenses of general assembly, insurance, banks and banking, penal and reformatory, roads and bridges, senatorial apportionment, world's fair, agriculture.

Salomon, Moses, (dem.), lawyer and manufacturer. Born in Peoria, Dec. 13, 1857, and four years later his father

MOSES SALOMON.

moved to Chicago with his family. Was educated in the common schools and at the Union College of Law in Chicago, after which he read law in

Allen C. Story's office and was admitted to the bar in '80. Is not married. Is president of the Chicago Architectural Iron Works, one of the largest industries of its kind in the United Sates; 150 men are employed. Is interested in legislation that will protect the people from the greed of monopolies and trusts, and advocates the opening of all markets to fair competition, and just and equal taxation. Senator Salomon is very popular among his constituents, having been elected in '92 in a strong republican district, the first democrat to break the republican majority, receiving 12,721 votes to 11,691 for Alexander White, rep.

Committees: Insurance (chairman), judiciary, railroads, corporations, public buildings, federal relations, congressional apportionment. license and miscellany, labor and manufactures, municipalities, revenue.

THOMAS H. SHERIDAN.

Sheridan, Thomas H., (rep.), Golconda; lawyer. Born in Pope county Dec. 16, 1860, and has had a hard row to hoe, but is now past the rockiest part of the journey of life. The senator's father died when he was 6 years old, leaving a widow and six children, two girls and four boys. It is said that he was born in a cave, and Pope county has many of them, his father being too poor to build a log hut on their rocky tract of land. About the time of the father's death the mother with her dependent little ones moved to Golconda, and for several years she took in washing and supported them the best she could, taking care that they attended school. In '71 the youngest son, then 9 years of age, was drowned, and in '76 the eldest, the then support of the family, met the same fate. The same year the second oldest went to California, and Senator Sheridan, then 16 years old, quit school and went to work in a spoke factory at $2 a week, and worked at that and in a brick yard and printing office until September, '79. The senator then received a teacher's certificate, taught school in the winter and ran a confectionery store in summer. Meantime he studied law, was admitted to practice in '83 and practiced and taught school for two years; was elected county superintendent of schools to fill a vacancy and re-elected in '86. Is married, and was elected senator in '90 over John Blanchard, dem., after a terrific fight by a vote of 6,104 to 5,974.

Committees: Judiciary, judicial department, finance and claims, education, elections, building and loan associations, state library, congressional apportionment.

Seibert, Peter, (dem.), Fayetteville; farmer. Born in the Grand Duchy of Hesse Darmstadt, April 24, 1844. Emigrated to America with his parents who moved on a farm 3½ miles east of Belleville in '52. There he was raised and educated, although he spent some time at the Belleville high school. Has been a member of the board of supervisors and was a member when St. Clair county was organized under township organization. Is married. Never sought an office and was elected senator in '90, receiving 6,054 votes to

PETER SEIBERT.

S. C. Smiley's (rep.) 4,951, running several hundred ahead of his ticket. Senator Seibert was a republican until '80, and began voting the democratic ticket in '82, the tariff policy of the republicans being too much for him. He has been a democrat ever since.

Committees: Charitable institutions chairman, revenue, appropriations, roads and bridges, agriculture, congressional apportionment, military, penal and reformatory, mines and mining, county and township organization.

Thiele, Emil, (dem.), Chicago; druggist. Born near Cologne on the Rhine, March 2, 1859, and emigrated to Chi-

EMIL THIELE.

cago soon after the great fire. Served for a time while a boy in a drug store, and graduated from the Chicago College of Pharmacy in '80. He has owned his present drug store on Archer avenue for about seven years, and has an interest in another one. Is not married. Was nominated as a representative of the strong German element in his district, and his popularity among his neighbors is attested by the fact that he was elected in '90 over Richard Burke, rep. and lab., the preceding senator, by a vote of 8,601 to 4,930. Senator Thiele has always voted with that element in the senate that has sought to restrict the powers and privileges of corporations and monopolies, although he does not go to an extreme. Is always in attendance.

Committees: Municipalities (chairman), judicial department, revenue, expenses of the general assembly, charitable institutions, penal and reformatory, education, elections, senatorial apportionment, library, labor and manufactures.

Wall, Hampton W., (dem.), Staunton; retired farmer. Born Nov. 10, 1832, on a farm near Staunton. Received a common school education. Is married. Has filled the offices of justice of the peace and member of the board of supervisors, and was a member of the House of Representatives in '77 and '79. Was elected to the state senate in '92 over James H. Hackett, rep., by a vote of 9,096 to 7,287, running ahead of his ticket. Senator Wall stands plump on the democratic platform and insists that all pledges ought to be fulfilled. The senator has made

HAMPTON W. WALL.

a strong fight this session for economy in the expenditure of public money.

Committees: Finance and claims (chairman), warehouses, revenue, appropriations, insurance, public buildings, roads and bridges, senatorial apportionment, building and loan associations, mines and mining, county and township organization, federal relations.

Wells, Albert W., (dem.), Quincy; lawyer. Born in South Woodstock, Conn., May 9, 1841. Received an academic education, and spent his early days on a farm. Taught school

ALBERT W. WELLS.

in New Jersey for several years, resigning to enlist in the Union army. Senator Wells took a full law course at Columbia college, and was admitted to

the bar in New York city. He moved to Quincy in '70, has been a successful lawyer ever since, and stands high at the bar. Has held various offices of trust, and has been a member of the board of education of Quincy for several years, and is president of the board now. Is a director and the attorney for the Ricker National bank, and holds a like position in the Quincy Gas company and other companies. Is married and has a family. Was elected to the house in '86 and again in '88; advanced to the senate in '90 practically without opposition, the republicans not naming a man against him. The senator has been a leader in every legislature of which he has been a member; was chairman of the house caucus in '89, and of the senate caucus in '91, and has served on the most important committees in both branches.

SAMUEL W. WRIGHT, JR.

Committees: Judicial department, (chairman), judiciary, railroads, appropriations, penal and reformatory, education, printing, elections, congressional apportionment, license and miscellany, labor and manufactures.

Wright, Samuel W., Jr., (dem.), Sullivan; farmer. Was born in Moultrie county, June 30, 1850, and is now an extensive farmer and stock raiser, owning a fine farm about three miles from Sullivan. Was educated in the public schools and finished in Bastian's Seminary, Sullivan, at that time an institution of considerable celebrity. Is a representative farmer, and has served several terms on the board of supervisors from Sullivan township, and was chairman most of the time. Is a good substantial representative of the farmer class in the legislature. Is married. Was elected to the senate in

'90, when the farmers' movement was rampant in Central Illinois, and when his district, usually reliably democratic, was in doubt; he polled 6,694 votes to 3,250 for Wm. G. Cochran, rep., and 3,107 for George Kincade, peo.

Committees: Railroads (chairman), public buildings and grounds (chairman), fees and salaries (chairman), judicial department, warehouses, appropriations, corporations, charitable institutions, senatorial apportionment, visit penal and reformatory, world's fair, agriculture, county and township organization.

LOUIS ZEARING.

Zearing, Louis, (rep.). Ladd; farmer. Born in Cumberland Co., Penn., Sept. 10, 1827, and moved with his parents to Bureau county in '36. Was educated in the district schools of primitive Illinois. One of his early experiences was the marketing in Chicago of a load of wheat taken to the embryo metropolis by ox team. In '50 he crossed the plains to California and in that state cast his first vote, for a republican, of course Winfield Scott for president in '52. Returning from California in '54, he married and began farming, and has held various local offices. Was elected to the senate in '90 by a vote of 5,018 to 4,641 for Simon Elliott, dem. Is one of the most reliable and industrious members, and is held in high esteem. Mr. Zearing never misses a session, and his record in the general assembly of '93, as well as in that of '91, will bear the closest investigation. The Senator is a staunch republican, and acts on his own judgment on all questions not of a purely party nature.

Committees: Expenses of general assembly, charitable institutions, penal and reformatory, public buildings, printing, roads and bridges, state library, canals and rivers, agriculture, labor and manufactures.

Taylor, Rev. Frederick Wm., D. D., Chaplain of the Senate, is the eldest son of Maj. Alfred Taylor, M. D., and Helen M. Leonard, and was born in Toledo, O., Jan. 11, 1853. Both his paternal and maternal grandfathers were army officers in the war of 1812, and his father was surgeon with the rank of major in the 2d O. Cav. during the late war from '61 to '63. Rev. Dr. Taylor's early life was passed in Cleveland, of which his grandfather Elisha Taylor, was one of the earliest settlers and most prominent citizens. Rev. Dr. Taylor graduated from Western Reserve University in '73 and from the General Theological Seminary in New York in '76. After two years' ministry in Ohio and New York, he was appointed Rector of Holy Trinity Parish, Danville, Ill., in '78, where he remained until Sept. '86, when he became Rector of St. Paul's Pro-Cathedral, in the See City of the Diocese, Springfield. Here he has led a busy life as a Parish Priest, and in the affairs of the Diocese as one of the Archdeacons, and as a member of various diocesan boards, and editor of the diocesan paper. He has sat in four successive General Conventions of the Episcopal church, as one of the Clinical Deputies from the Diocese of Springfield, and has taken an active part in the debates and legislation of that dignified body. He is the first

CHAPLAIN TAYLOR.

Priest of the Episcopal Church who has been Chaplain of the Senate. He is a strict churchman in religion, and a democrat in politics. He is a plain, clear and forcible preacher, and is well known in his church as a trenchant writer.

THE SPEAKER.

The Speaker of the House of Representatives, Hon. Clayton E. Crafts, is now serving his sixth consecutive term as a member of the lower branch of the general assembly, having been elected in '82, '84, '86, '88, '90, '92. This is his second term as speaker—the only two sessions when his party has been in a clear majority in the house since 1863. Mr. Crafts was born in Auburn, Geanga Co., O., July 8, 1848. His father and his grandfather were far-

of the Iroquois Club and the County Democracy, and is one of the most skillful leaders in the state. As a parliamentarian he is the peer of any man. He was the candidate of the democrats for speaker in the session of '87, and also in '89, '91, and '93, and has been regarded as the democratic leader in every session after his first. He is earnest, incisive and forcible in debate, and there is no one to compete with him in shrewd manipulation of parliamentary law. As speaker his fairness and impartiality are conceded even by his political enemies. To Mr.

mers, and the latter was about the only man in his neighborhood that was capable of drawing up legal documents while the former was the only democrat in Auburn for many years. Mr. Crafts was educated at Hiram College, one of the most famous educational institutions of Ohio, and is a graduate of the Cleveland Law School, and was admitted to the bar in '68. A portion of his legal study was pursued in the office of John J. Van Allen, a celebrated lawyer and politician of New York. He moved to Chicago in '69, and has had a most extraordinarily successful practice ever since. He is a member of the Presbyterian church,

Crafts more than any man is due the credit for the successful contest made by the democrats in the last general assembly for the election of Gen. Palmer to the United States senate.

As a delegate to state and national democratic conventions Mr. Crafts has had a great deal to do in shaping the policy of his party, as well as selecting candidates for the endorsement of the people. He is a strict party man, and believes in a strong organization of his party in the legislature, with a rigorous espionage on those who neglect their duties. Mr. Crafts lives in the suburban village of Austin, in Cook county, is married and well to do.

HALL OF THE HOUSE.

THE HOUSE.

The House of Representatives consists of 153 members elected every two years. They receive $5 per diem during the session, $50 for stationery and 10 cents a mile for the actual distance from their homes to the state capitol. The present house of representatives was chosen in November, 1892, and consists of 78 democrats and 75 republicans, with the seat of Mr. Bish, republican, of Chicago, contested by Sol Van Praag, democrat. Hon. Ernst Meyer died in Springfield May 11, '93.

Biographies marked thus * are not accompanied by portraits.

It is fortunate that the executive officers of the house are intelligent and cool-headed. Otherwise the journals would exhibit evidences of some of the exciting scenes enacted on the floor, and the confusion and wrangles that take place frequently would end in broken heads. Speaker Crafts, Clerk Ross, Doorkeeper Browne, Assistant Doorkeeper Rives and their assistants are good officers, reliable and courteous. The house is generally a placid body, but occasionally a storm breaks on the floor that bids fair to annihilate many members.

THE STEERING COMMITTEES.

Indispensable in the conduct of a campaign in which party advantages are to be won or lost through legislative action, are the advisory or "steering" committees of each party. The leadership is entrusted to these committees for the session, and the rank and file are expected to obey orders, even to the point of resigning their seats. In the senate these committees are made up thus:

Democrats: Caldwell (chairman), Mahoney, Craig, Salomon and Green.

Republicans: Berry (chairman), Bass, Aspinwall, Sheridan and Knopf.

The house steering committees are composed of the following:

Democrats: McKinlay (chairman), Morris, Johnson of Whiteside, Wilson of Ogle, O'Donnell, McInerney, Donnelly, Smith of Livingston, Merritt, Carson, Ferns and Farrell.

Republicans: Hawley (chairman), Paddock, Warder, Anderson of Henderson, Meyer of Cook, O'Connell, McKnight, Langhenry, Berry.

Ross, Robert W., (dem.), Vandalia; real estate dealer and Clerk of the House. Was born in Fayette county, Dec. 31, 1843, of Scotch-Welsh parents, who moved to Illinois from Kentucky. He was educated in the common schools and at Tuscarora Academy, Penn., which he left in March '63 to enter the county clerk's office of Fayette county. He entered the army, enlisting in Co. E, 143d Ill. Inf.; was mustered out in '64 and resumed his position in the county clerk's office. After a year he went into the drug business and kept it up for three years, when he sold out and became a deputy in the circuit clerk's office. He was elected clerk of the House of Representatives in '75, and was elected circuit clerk of Fayette county in '76, and re-elected in '80— eight years in all Then he served

CLERK ROSS.

two more years in his successor's office. He was appointed by President Cleveland recorder-general of the land office and resigned when President Harrison assumed charge. Has since been engaged in the real estate business. He was nominated for clerk of the house last January by acclamation in the democratic caucus. He is not married and own 160 acres of land.

Browne, Edgar S., Doorkeeper of the House, of Mendota, was born in Mason, Me., May, 11, 1851, and is a lawyer by profession. Mr. Browne was educated at the Norway, (Me.) Normal Institute, and graduated from Gould's Academy, Bethel, and the State Normal School at Farmington; was admitted to the bar in '70, when he was 20 years old. Practiced at Portland for five years, and moved to Chicago, where he remained for a year, and in '77 moved to LaSalle county. He was State Commissioner of Deeds in Maine; has been city attorney of Mendota, and was a member of the house of representatives in

DOORKEEPER BROWNE.

Illinois in '87 and '89; was chosen doorkeeper of the house in '91, and was again complimented last January, and has organized a system for each branch under him, so that all the employes under his supervision discharge their duties without friction. In the session of '89 he succeeded as a member of the house in getting the Chicago Drainage scheme amended so as to protect the Illinois Valley people. He is married and has two children.

CONRAD A. AMBROSIUS.

Ambrosius, Conrad A., (dem.), Collinsville; merchant. Born in Hesse Cassel, Germany, Jan. 18, 1839, and emigrated to America in Jan. '41 with his parents, arriving at New Orleans and coming up the Mississippi, the route all western settlers took in the early days, there being no railroads, and travel overland being attended with difficulties and dangers. His parents stopped in St. Louis until Jan. '49 and then moved to what is now Collinsville, an Indian transporting the family with four oxen. Mr. Ambrosius has lived near and in Collinsville ever since. His education was limited; he hardly knew what a public school was, and obtained most of his education by his own efforts. He remained on the farm until '74, when he went into the coal business, being elected president and general superintendent of the Canteen Coal Mining Co. He continued in this until '87, when he sold out and went into the real estate business. He afterwards opened a

JAMES J. ANDERSON.

general merchandise store under the firm name of Ambrosius & Sons, and it is one of the most substantial concerns in the city, doing a large and safe business. Is married and financially independent of the world. Has been supervisor for several years, was alderman fourteen years, and has held other offices. He was nominated for representative a little against his will, but like a true democrat, bowed to the will of the party and accepted, making a thorough and successful canvass. He never sought an office in his life.

Committees: Mines and mining, public charities, building and loan associations, retrenchment, drainage, soldiers' home, farm drainage.

Anderson, James J., (dem.), Nashville; lawyer. Born in Nottoway Co., Va., Dec. 15, 1849, and moved with his father to St. Louis two years later, remaining there until he was 23. He was educated in the public schools of St. Louis and the City University. He moved to Richview, Ill., in '72, and learned telegraphy, accepting a place on the Iron Mountain railroad in Missouri. He read law in Richview and in his new position when his duties did not demand his attention, and was admitted to the bar in '75, beginning the practice of his profession at Glasgow, Mo. In '76 he moved to Nashville, bought The Democrat from Forman Brothers, and run it in connection with his legal business until last July, when he sold the paper and devoted himself entirely to his profession. He has been master in chancery of Washington county for many years, and was city attorney of Nashville for a term. He made The Democrat second to none in power and standing while he had charge of it, and stands very close to Col. Morrison, Congressman Forman and other prominent democratic leaders in the state. He has been one of the ruling spirits in the Illinois Press association, and the Southern Illinois Press association. Is married.

Committees: Penal and reformatory (chairman), congressional apportionment, judiciary, judicial department, finance, retrenchment.

Anderson, James O., (rep.), Decorra; farmer. Born in Henderson county,

JAMES O. ANDERSON.

Aug. 1, 1845, was raised on a farm, received a common school education, and left Monmouth College when a student to enlist in the 28th Ill. Inf., in which he attained the rank of second lieutenant. Returning from the war he married and engaged in farming, which is his present occupation. He was sheriff of Henderson county for ten years, and gained considerable notoriety by the pursuit of two desperadoes, one of whom being taken to Durand, Wis., was lynched. He was elected to the house in '88, '90, and '92. His value as a legislator has been increased with

MICHAEL BARTON.

each return to the house, and he is influential and popular with his colleagues.

Committees: Agriculture, to visit penal and reformatory institutions, world's fair, congressional apportionment, steering committee.

*****Armstrong, Fowler A.**, (rep.), Massac Creek; teacher and farmer. Born in Massac county, March 18, 1847. Served on the Tennessee and Cumberland rivers on a gun-boat during the war. Was county superintendent of schools from '84 to '88, and was elected to the house in '90 and '92. Is married and owns 160 acres of land.

Committees: County and township organization, agriculture, federal relations, soldiers' home, horticulture.

Barton, Michael, (dem.), Spring Valley; bank cashier. Born in County Kerry, Ireland, Sept. 1, 1834, and came to America in '49 with his parents, who settled in Kentucky. Moved to Illinois in '54. Learned the trade of a harness maker, and worked at it for some time. In '64 accepted a place as clerk in the Rock Island railroad offices at Ottawa; was promoted to be station agent of the same road at La Salle in '66, and in '86 he resigned to accept the position of cashier of the Spring Valley National bank. He is one of the best and most reliable members of the legislature. Is married. Was elected to the house in '90 and again in '92. He bent his energies in the last legislature towards the enactment of an arbitration law that would prevent strikes.

Committees: Mines and mining (chairman), canal-river improvement and commerce, penal and reformatory, manufactures, state and municipal indebtedness, insurance.

Baldwin, Leverett S., (dem.), Windsor; farmer. Born in Hinesburg, Vt., Oct. 28, 1839, and is self-educated. Was with the I. & St. L. R. R. as train boy, brakeman, baggageman and freight conductor. Moved to Windsor 27 years ago, and has held minor offices. Is married and owns 500 acres of land.

Committees: Railroads, live stock and dairying, labor and industrial affairs, judicial department, drainage, farm drainage, Wann investigation (special.)

Beals, Reuben F., (rep.), Galva; farmer. Born near Cleveland, O., Aug. 12, 1832, and for nineteen years he lived there, working on the farm and attending district school as opportunity offered. He started out for himself at 19, as a woodchopper, which he followed for a short time, and then learned the carpenter trade. He was a good workman, clever with his tools and industrious, and soon branched into business for himself, taking contracts to erect houses. In '55 he emigrated to Oneida, Ill., and a year later moved into Clover township, where he lived for 36 years. He built houses for

REUBEN F. BEALS.

his neighbors for two years, and in '58 bought 80 acres and began farming. By close application, economy and hard work he has accumulated 250 acres of splendid land. In Aug. '62 he enlisted in Co. I, 102d Ill. Inf., and participated in all the battles of the Atlanta campaign, serving faithfully for three years and receiving one wound; he commanded a company several times. He returned to the farm after the war. He is an Odd Fellow, a Mason, and is past commander of Holden Post, G. A. R. He was a supervisor for six years, and is mar-

ROBERT J. BECK.

ried. He was a member of the legislature of '91, and is highly regarded by his colleagues.

Committees: State institutions, county and township organization, state and municipal indebtedness, senatorial apportionment.

Beck, Robert J., (rep.), Chemung; contractor and builder. Born in County Armagh, Ireland, Dec. 17, 1851, and emigrated with his parents to America in '52, going direct to McHenry county, where he has been ever since. He was educated in the common schools. Has been justice of the peace for twenty years and supervisor for ten years, and his long service justifies the statement that he was a faithful servant of the people. Was elected to the house in the spring of '89 to fill the vacancy caused by the death of E. M. Haines, dem. He is married and owns 140 acres of land. Mr. Beck is not an orator, but accomplishes more by hard work in committee rooms than many a man with a loud voice and rhetorical effects.

Committees: Canal-river improvement and commerce, state institutions, public buildings, fish and game, farm drainage.

Berry, Daniel S., (rep.), Savanna; lawyer. Born in Sterling, Ill., May 13, 1858, and educated in the public schools. Taught school for four years in Whiteside county, read law at Morrison and was admitted to practice in

'82. The following spring he located at Savanna, where he has had a very successful career. He has been city attorney of Savanna and president of the board of education. He has always

DANIEL S. BERRY.

eloquently contended that children should be compelled to attend school, and compelled to learn the English language, and is a staunch friend of the public schools of Illinois. Is married. Was elected to the house in '90, and re-elected in '92. Is one of the republican leaders in the legislature and stands high in party councils in the Illinois. He introduced and forced through the house a bill prohibiting pool selling in the state.

JAMES E. BISH.

Committees: Judiciary, railroads, education, elections, libraries, steering committee.

Bish, James E., (rep.), Chicago; real estate. Born in St. Francis Co., Mo., of slave parents, Oct. 1, 1859, and after many wanderings settled in Chicago in '81. He received a common school education, principally in the Belleville schools. Is married. He began hustling for himself when he was 11 years old, and was night clerk of the Commercial hotel at Alton for several years; studied law with Judge Alex. W. Hope for a time; learned telegraphy, and finally went to Chicago, where he worked for Price's Baking Powder Co. for nine years, and has held his present position with F. C. Vierling, real estate agent, for over a year. He has dabbled in politics to some extent, but never held a political office until last year, when he was sanitary policeman for his ward. His seat is being contested by Sol Van Praag, dem. He is writing "The Past, Present and Future of the Negro," and the

J. EDWIN BLACK.

work is nearing completion. It will be an important addition to historical literature.

Committees: Manufactures, state institutions, contingent expenses, state and municipal indebtedness.

Black, J. Edwin, (dem.), Bridgeport; farmer. Born in Lawrence county, March 10, 1846, and was raised on a farm with all its disadvantages in early days and its hard work. Educated in the country schools, and at 19 taught school for a time. Then he went to Shurtleff College, finished his education, returned home and again taught school for three years. He then entered the circuit clerk's office as chief deputy, remaining three years. During President Johnson's administration he was a clerk in the treasury department at Washington. He returned to Illinois in '69, married and settled down on a farm, where he has been ever since, respected by all. When Dr. Lyon resigned his seat in the house in '90 to accept a postoffice, Mr. Black was elected to fill the vacancy, and he was re-elected in '92. He has always discharged his duties like an honest man, and to the best of his ability. Is married, and owns over 300 acres of land. He is especially interested in legislation that will benefit farmers, in the way of improved roads, and his sympathies lean toward the weaker classes, for he favors a reform school for girls and charitable institutions for the needy.

Committees: Senatorial apportionment (chairman), agriculture, visit charitable institutions, drainage, libraries, executive department, horticulture.

Brandt, John N., (dem.), Polo; farmer and stock raiser. Born in Washington Co., Md., Aug. 26, 1851, and moved with his parents to Illinois in '61, settling in Ogle county, near Forreston. A year later they moved to Carroll county, where he now lives, although his postoffice is in Ogle. He was educated in the common schools and taught school for one year. Then he went into the windmill, pump and well business, following it successfully for ten years. He ran a democratic newspaper in Morrison for some time The Dispatch—and during the campaign of '80 made things lively for the

JOHN N. BRANDT.

republicans with his Campaign Democrat. In '81 he returned to farming and stock raising. He is not married and owns over 200 acres of fine land. He has been a school trustee ever since he went to Carroll county, and was elected supervisor one term when the township was four to one republican. He is interested in raising Morgan horses and Chester White hogs, and owns splendid specimens of each. He is always in attendance.

Committees: Military affairs (chairman), state institutions, agriculture, executive department, roads and bridges, soldiers' home.

CHARLES P. BRYAN.

Bryan, Charles P., (rep.), Elmhurst; city address, University club, Chicago; journalist. Born in Chicago, Oct. 2, 1855. Was educated at the University of Virginia and the Columbia Law School; was admitted to practice in '78, and in '79 moved to Colorado. Was elected to the legislature of that state in '80, and was urged for higher preferment. Returned to Chicago in '83 and has since lead a literary life. Was a member of Gov. Oglesby's and Gov. Fifer's military staff also of Gov. Altgeld's with the rank of colonel, having previously served in the 1st regiment, I. N. G., and in the Guard of Colorado. Elected to the Illinois legislature in '90 and re-elected in '92. Is deeply interested in the success of the World's Columbian Exposition and in military matters. Is not married. He is on several important committees.

Mr. Bryan is independent in his actions, except on party questions when he bows to the will of the majority.

*****Bonney, Joel W.**, (dem.), Quincy; physician. Born in Strong, Maine, Feb. 23, 1828. In '48 he moved to Clark Co., Mo., where he remained until the fall of '59, when he went to Quincy. His education was meagre. Graduated from the State Medical University, St. Louis, in '57. Is married.

Committees: Education, fish and game, banks and banking, public charities.

Burke, William, (dem.), Chicago; wholesale wine and liquor dealer. Born in Chicago June 15, 1859, and educated in the public schools. He learned the trade of a carpenter early in life, and

WILLIAM BURKE.

followed it for five years. Then he went into the wholesale liquor business, and has been engaged in it for nine years. He is interested in three establishments in Chicago, and does a large business. He is not married, and is comfortably well off in this world's goods. He was elected to the house in '90, and was returned in '92, running ahead of his ticket nearly 2,500 votes. Was a member of important committees in the session of '91,

PETER CAHILL.

and is especially interested in labor legislation, but looks after the interests of the people regardless of their station.

Committees: Warehouses (chairman), municipal corporations, railroads, sanitary affairs, roads and bridges, revenue, live stock and dairying.

Cahill, Peter, (dem.), Brimfield; farmer. Born in County Meath, Ireland, Feb. 12, 1843, and came to Illinois with his parents, landing at New Orleans and taking the Mississippi and Illinois rivers to Peoria, arriving in June '47, where he has lived and farmed all his life. He was educated in the common schools. Has been a member of the board of supervisors for the last fourteen years, and for the last three years he has been chairman of the board, a position which he now fills to the credit of himself and his township. He is not married, and owns 500 acres of Peoria land, and there is none richer on the face of the globe; he accumulated it all himself by industry, frugality and intelligent farming. He

ETHELBERT CALLAHAN.

is honest and straightforward in his dealings with his fellowman, and possesses the confidence of the people of Peoria.

Committees: Canal-river improvement and commerce, roads and bridges, sanitary affairs warehouses, farm drainage, history-geology and science.

Callahan, Ethelbert, (rep.), Robinson; lawyer. Born near Newark, O., Dec. 17, 1829, and educated in the public schools. In '49 he moved to Crawford County, Ill., and for two years farmed in summer and taught school in winter; another year was spent as clerk in a general store; then for a year he was editor of The Wabash Sentinel, and during the campaign of '54 he edited The Marshall Telegraph, the only anti-democratic paper in his congressional district. He joined the republicans and entered into the Fremont campaign with ardor. His speeches were bold and uncompromising, and attracted wide attention. In '60 he was the recognized leader of the republicans of Southern Illinois, and in '64 he was his party's candidate for congress. Gov. Oglesby appointed him a member of the first state board of equalization; he was also a member of the house in '75, which was controlled by the independents; in '80 was an elector at large, and in '88 a district elector. Was admitted to the bar when past 30 years of age, and was president of the state bar association in '89. In '90 he was elected to the house again, and returned in '92. In the session of '91 he offered an amendment in the house to the Australian election bill permitting laboring men to be absent from work for two hours without loss of pay on election day. He is championing this session a bill to protect brakemen, by compelling railroads to block their switches and frogs. He is one of the ablest and best members of the general assembly. Is married and comfortably wealthy.

Committees: Judiciary, revenue, retrenchment, senatorial apportionment.

Campbell, Albert, (rep.), Effingham; dry goods merchant. Born Nov. 1, 1855, in Somerset, O., and was educated in the common schools, at the same time working at whatever he

ALBERT CAMPBELL.

could get to do. He moved to Effingham in '71, and worked in a planing mill in St. Louis in '74. Returning to Effingham in '87, he married and settled down for good. He is regarded with respect by the people of Effingham, and is liberal and popular. He has always been a strong, hustling republican, and has contributed of time and money towards the success of his party. Mr. Campbell gives the steering committee no trouble, for he is always present during sessions.

Committees: Revenue, finance, sanitary affairs, roads and bridges, public charities.

DANIEL A. CAMPBELL.

Campbell, Daniel A., (rep.), Chicago; lawyer. Born in Elgin June 23, 1863, and was educated in the common schools and at the Chicago Union College of Law. Was admitted to the bar in '86, and has been in active practice ever since, principally in the real estate and commercial lines. Has met with very flattering success in his legal career. Is not married, and this is the first office he ever held. He is held in high esteem by his colleagues, and is a hard worker in committees. Mr. Campbell is one of the youngest members, and one of the most diligent and best informed. He performs his duties unostentatiously, but creditably to himself, his party and his constituents. In Cook county politics he is an active and effective worker. He believes in a strong party organization of the republican members of the general assembly.

Committees: Judicial department, municipal corporations, education, fees and salaries, fish and game.

Carlin, Stephen E., (dem.), Canton; lawyer. Born in Fulton county, Feb. 8, 1849. Educated in the public schools and at Ann Arbor University, graduating in '68. Then he taught school until he got tired of it, stood an examination for admission to the bar, and passed in '77. He has been practicing with decided success ever since. Is married and possessed of a comfortable competence. Mr. Carlin never held public office before, but made a splendid campaign of the state in '90 for the democratic state central com-

STEPHEN E. CARLIN.

mittee. He does not talk to the press gallery, and is never on his feet unless he has got something to say. He has taken a prominent place in the house and is a radical in politics but conservative in other matters.

Committees: Judiciary, miscellaneous subjects, mines and mining, state institutions, farm drainage, fish and game.

Carmody, Henry P., (dem.), Chicago; contractor. Born in Simcoe, Canada, March 19, 1861, and moved with his

HENRY P. CARMODY.

parents to Chicago three months later. Received a common school education until 12 years old, when he began to earn his own living by working in the brick yards, packing houses and lumber yards of Chicago. Is married. Was elected to the house in '88, re-elected in '90 and again in '92 by increased majorities. He is industrious as a legislator and one of the hardest workers in Chicago for the democratic ticket. He is very popular with his constituents, and has been on some of the most important committees in the house every session.

Committees: Labor and industrial affairs (chairman), corporations, municipal corporations, senatorial apportionment, canal-river improvement and commerce, public buildings and others of less importance.

Carson, Thomas B., (dem.), Urbana; salesman. Born in Urbana, Ill., March 6, 1843, and received a good common school education. He was reared on a farm and left the harvest field in '61 to join the 25th Ill. Inf., with which he

THOMAS B. CARSON.

served to the close of the war. He is an uncompromising democrat, and has been an active participant in the campaigns in eastern Illinois for years. In '85 he was elected doorkeeper of the house by the democrats, and during the fierce Morrison-Logan senatorial contest, he filled the position with dignity and to the entire satisfaction of everybody. During Cleveland's first term he was a special agent of the internal revenue department. Is married. Was elected to the house in '90 and again in '92, and in both sessions has taken an active part in legislation. In the session of '91 Mr. Carson was assigned to important committees.

Committees: Banks and banking (chairman), municipal corporations, federal relations, history-geology and science, drainage, enrolled and engrossed bills, steering committee.

Carter, Robert S., (dem.), Petersburg; fire insurance. Was born in La Grange, Fayette Co., Texas, July 26, 1855, and moved to Petersburg in '73. He received his education in the public

ROBERT S. CARTER.

and private schools of Texas. Is married. He began life for himself in '70 as a drug clerk, filling prescriptions until '73. He was deputy circuit clerk of Menard county for four years, from '73 to '77, and then he went into the abstract, loan, real estate and insurance business at Petersburg, and has been exclusively in the line of general insurance since '81. Is master in chancery of Menard county now. Mr. Carter is a staunch democrat and is always in his seat.

GEORGE S. CAUGHLAN.

Committees: Insurance, education, appropriations, claims, fish and game, and others of less importance.

Caughlan, George S., (rep.). Trenton; student of law. Born in St. Louis Jan. 22, 1865, and is a son of a Methodist minister, whose duties as a minister of the gospel necessitated a frequent change of residence, and Mr. Caughlan acquired a good common education in various cities of Southern Illinois. He entered McKendree College at Lebanon, when he made up for lost time by energy and application. Although a member of the legislature, he is now taking a course of law at that college. Is married and has held several minor offices. He is an incisive speaker, and when he claims the floor, which is not often, he commands the attention of the house. He is too young to have a record in the past, but bids fair to carve out a promising future. He displayed considerable ability in the debate on the report of the special committee to investigate the Wann disaster.

CHARLES T. CHERRY.

Committees: Judicial department, warehouses, mines and mining, building and loan associations, miscellaneous, executive department, to investigate the Wann disaster (special).

Cherry, Charles T., (rep.). Oswego; farmer. Born in Oswego Feb. 20, 1858, and was educated in the public schools. He owns a magnificent tract of Kendall county land, which he farms himself, and on which he raises fine Poland-China hogs, Cotswold sheep and road and draft horses. He is popular with his colleagues on both sides of the house; is always at his seat, and is particularly interested in legislation affecting the farmer, stock raiser and republican party. Was elected to the house in '90, and again in '92. Is married and has one son. Mr. Cherry takes an active interest in legislation.

and his value increases with his length of service.

Committees: Corporations, live stock and dairying, banks and banking, agriculture, loan and homestead associations.

Claggett, Bernard J., (dem.), Lexington; banker. Born in Lexington, Feb. 12, 1861, and is indebted to the careful and systematic training of his father for his success as a man. He was educated at Wesleyan University, and at Notre Dame, Ind., taking the literary course at the latter; graduated at Jones' Commercial College, St. Louis, in '80. Then he returned home and entered his father's store as clerk. In '82 he was admitted to the firm, and in December, when the First National Bank was organized, he was made cashier, a position he has held ever since. In addition to his connection with the bank and the large business interests of his father's estate, he is largely interested in farming, stock raising, and is a partner in the mercantile business of Claggett Bros. & Co., and Claggett & Stevens, liverymen. In '88 he was elected to the city council, and although the youngest member, was made president, which office he filled with much credit. When the city reorganized he was chosen first mayor without opposition, and was honored by a unanimous re-election. He resigned to take his seat in the house, but the council refused to accept it. He has always been a democrat, and always took a

BERNARD J. CLAGGETT.

deep interest in politics, contributing liberally to the campaign. Is married and owns considerable valuable land.

Committees: Printing (chairman), penal and reformatory, banks and banking, state and municipal indebtedness, claims, military, world's fair.

Clark, William O., (rep.), Peoria; hotel proprietor. Born in Lynn, Mass., Jan. 18, 1844, and was associated with his father in the hotel business up to the time of the death of the latter. He has been proprietor of hotels in Rock Island, Geneseo, Mattoon, Bushnell, Charleston, Springfield, Bloom-

WILLIAM O. CLARK.

ington and Peoria, and is well known to the traveling public. Received a public school education, and is married. Enlisted in Co. A, 143d Ill. Inf., and was in the army of the southwest. He has been a member of the city council of Peoria, and is interested in the welfare of his constituents, and it can be said that a better servant Peoria never sent to Springfield. He is an Elk, a Modern Woodman and a member of the Royal League.

Committees: Railroads, agriculture, canal-river improvement and commerce, state and municipal indebtedness, claims.

Conway, Bryan, (dem.), Chicago; employed by Armour & Co. Born in Chicago, Oct. 14, 1861, and has grown up as one of the most popular young democrats in his district, being especially liked by the laboring men. Received a fair education at the public and parochial schools of Chicago. He has been employed in nearly every department of Armour's & Co.'s great butchering and packing establishment, and has held responsible positions with that firm for the last twelve years. Was elected to the house in '90, and again in '92 by an increased majority. During both sessions he took a prominent part in all legislation, being especially active on measures that concerned Cook county and his own constituents. He is one of the most effective workers in the democratic party in Cook county. He is married an in independent circumstances financially.

BRYAN CONWAY.

Committees: sanitary affairs (chairman), railroads, warehouses, municipal corporations, canal-river improvement and commerce

Creighton, Thomas H., (rep.), Fairfield; teacher. Born on a farm in Wayne county, Nov. 29, 1865, and was educated in the common schools and at Hayward Collegiate Institute in Fairfield, graduating in the class of '90. He is too young to have a political record and does not seek one, being quiet and retiring. His tastes rather

THOMAS H. CREIGHTON.

run in the direction of literature and learning. He was superintendent of the Fairfield city schools for two years, resigning on his nomination to the house. He was named by acclamation in the republican convention last spring. He is very anxious for the passage of a uniform text book bill, and is a hard working, conscientious member who can be relied on to be in his seat during sessions. Is not married.

Committees: Education, fees and salaries, history-geology and science, libraries, executive department.

Cusey, John, (rep.), mechanic; Farmer City. Born in Richland Co., O., April 9, 1822, and moved to McLean Co., Ill., in '36, and to DeWitt county in '83, and has lived there ever since. He is a self-educated man, having no chance to attend the district schools of his native state. He has a good common school education, however, thanks to his ambition and pluck. He is married, and was state senator from '72 to '76, and member of the state board of

JOHN CUSEY.

equalization from '80 to '84. He has been township assessor nine times, and member of the county board for both McLean and DeWitt counties, representing the latter now. Mr. Cusey was a member of the first republican state convention, which met in Bloomington in '54, and nominated Jesse O. Norton of Will county for congress, the first republican congressman from Illinois. In the same convention he seconded a resolution that named the new party "Republican." He has always voted in opposition to the democratic party.

Committees: Revenue, drainage, federal relations, history-geology and science.

*****Dazey, Mitchell,** (dem.), Lima; farmer. Born in Bourbon Co., Ky., Oct. 2, 1820. Educated in common schools, and was elected to the house in '89 to fill a vacancy. Is married and owns 305 acres of land.

Committees: Drainage, farm drainage, retrenchment, appropriations, libraries.

*****Dean, William C.**, (dem.), Ava; miller and farmer. Born in Randolph Co., Ill., Dec. 10, 1838, and moved to Ava in '76. Was educated in the common schools; was in the mercantile business until two years ago, when he purchased a roller mill. Is married and owns 3,000 acres of land.

Committees: Agriculture, to visit educational institutions, state institutions, roads.

Dearborn, Luther M., (dem.), Aurora: lawyer. Born at Geneva, Ill., Aug. 5, 1858, and educated at Bishop Whipple's School, Fairbault, Minn., and at Racine, Wis. He read law in the office of Hon. John N. Jewett; afterwards

LUTHER M. DEARBORN.

spent two years at Harvard Law School, and was admitted to practice in '82. He remained in Chicago for three years in the law office of his father, Hon. Luther Dearborn, and John B. Cohrs, and then formed a partnership with Judge Annis in Aurora. Is not married. He was elected to the house in '90 and again in '92, and in both he held important committee assignments.

Committees: Roads and bridges (chairman), judiciary, railroads, manufactures, insurance, contingent expenses, to investigate the sweat shop evil (special).

Deneen, Charles S., (rep.), Chicago; lawyer. Born in Edwardsville May 4, 1863, and moved to Chicago in the fall of '85. He was educated at McKendree College, Lebanon, in which institution his father was a professor for nearly thirty years. Mr. Deneen graduated in law in '85 and was admitted to the bar in Jan. '87, and has had a very successful and profitable practice ever since. Is married and this is his first office. He taught in a

CHARLES S. DENEEN.

night school in Chicago for three years. Was attorney for Representative Bish in the contested election case of VanPraag vs. Bish, and his skillful handling of the case attracted the attention of the older political leaders. Mr. Deneen is a young man with flattering prospects for a splendid future, and is highly regarded by those who know him.

Committees: Corporations, drainage, judicial department, labor and industrial affairs, to investigate the sweat shop evil.

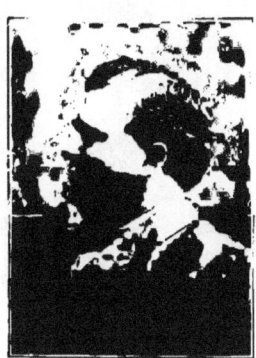

JOHN C. DONNELLY.

Donnelly, John C., (dem.); Woodstock; clerk. Was born in Woodstock, Nov. 3, 1855, and educated in the common schools with a finishing course at Notre Dame. For two years he was clerk in the office of the circuit clerk of McHenry county. He also has represented the Northwestern railroad in the south. He was deputy collector of internal revenue under Cleveland. Mr. Donnelly is one of the most popular and affable members of the general assembly. Was elected to the house in '90, and although the district is the strongest republican district in the state and an independent democrat was running against him he received more votes than either of the republicans or the independent. He is the first democrat that has been returned from the district a second time immediately following the first. He is very influential in northern Illinois democratic politics, and takes a prominent part in all important legislation.

Committees: Corporations (chairman), banks and banking, live stock and dairying, sanitary affairs, insurance, miscellaneous subjects, enrolled and engrossed bills, senatorial apportionment, steering committee.

Douglas, John J., (rep.), Chester; farmer. Born in Chester Aug. 17, 1849, and was educated in the common schools and McKendree College. Then he learned the trade of miller. His parents came from Scotland and when he was 22 years old he visited the crags and moors of the Land of the Thistle. Returning home he married

JOHN J. DOUGLAS.

in '72, bought a farm and settled down, and has farmed ever since. In this occupation he has been successful, owing more to his own intelligence and industry than to the fertility of the soil. He owns 340 acres of good land, and is one of the most reliable and substantial members of the house.

Committees: Mines and mining, fees and salaries, roads and bridges, horticulture.

Dow, Augustus, (rep.), Pittsfield; flour manufacturer. Born in South Coventry, Tolland county, Connecticut, Oct. 9, 1841, and in '58 moved to Pittsfield, where he has lived ever

AUGUSTUS DOW.

since. He received an academic education in his native town and from '62 to '65 was connected with the pay department of the United States army. After the war he returned to Pittsfield and engaged in the mercantile business, continuing it until '70, when he sold out and started the manufacture of flour on a large scale. Pittsfield is a democratic district, but he has been elected to the county board several times, and mayor of the city four years. Mr. Dow has been connected with all the improvements of a local nature, and is regarded as one of the foremost and most liberal citizens. He is an uncompromising republican, is a director in the First National Bank and is married.

Committees: Canal-river improvement and commerce, drainage, state and municipal indebtedness, to visit charitable institutions.

***Drury, Joseph W.**, (dem.), Waterloo; farmer and dairyman. Born in St. Louis Feb. 5, 1832, and educated at McKendree College. Moved with his parents to Monroe county when three years old; was provost marshal of Monroe county during the war. Was sheriff from '66 to '74, excepting two years; has held several school offices, is married and owns 645 acres.

Committees: Congressional apportionment, world's fair, horticulture, fees and salaries, penal and reformatory, live stock.

*Duncan, John H., (rep.), Marion; teacher. Born in Marshall Co., Ky., June 27, 1858, and moved with his parents to Williamson county in '65. Educated at Shurtleff College; taught school 3 years; elected county superintendent of schools in '82 and '86; elected to the house in '90 and '92; married.

Committees: Mines and mining, revenue, labor, license, senatorial apportionment.

*Dyer, John, (rep.), Fulton; shoemaker. Born in Jefferson Co., N. Y., March 6, 1824. Enlisted in Co. F 52d Ill. and Co. F 93d Ill. Inf. Received a meager education, is married and has been justice of the peace and on the county board 16 years.

Committees: State institutions, public buildings, soldiers' home.

Edmiston, John D., (rep.), Olney; merchant and farmer. Born in Richland county June 13, 1861, and was educated in the Olney high school, after which he learned the painter's trade, and then went into the mercantile business with his father. This he sold out and is now running a fruit farm of apples and peaches. Is married. Has been an alderman and has held other minor offices. He is an Odd Fellow, a Modern Woodman and an A. O. U. W. He didn't seek the nomination last year for his present office, nevertheless was chosen by acclamation and ran 500 ahead of his ticket; has been in politics and a delegate to state conventions ever since he voted.

JOHN D. EDMISTON.

Mr. Edmiston is constant in attendance and informs himself on the merits of every measure that comes up.

Committees: Railroads, state institutions, manufactures, sanitary affairs, enrolled and engrossed bills, horticulture.

Ellsworth, Urbin S., (rep.), Deer Park, LaSalle Co.; farmer. Born in South Ottawa, April 19, 1851, and five years later his parents moved to Deer Park township. He completed his education at Jennings Seminary, Aurora, graduating in the classical course in '74. Two years afterwards

URBIN S. ELLSWORTH.

he married. Has represented his township three times on the board of supervisors. Is a member of the Farmers Alliance, and is a loyal republican. He received his political education from his grandfather, John Clark, who was dismissed from church in '39 because of his abolition views. Was elected to the house in '90 and '92. In the session of '91 he strongly advocated a bill for an insane hospital northwest of the Illinois river, in order to relieve the county poor houses of their insane charges. He is interested especially in legislation that affects the Illinois river valley.

Committees: Corporations, education, revenue, agriculture, sanitary affairs, insurance.

Erickson, Samuel E., (rep.), Chicago; deputy sheriff. Born in Lindkoping, Sweden, March 4, 1860; parents emigrated to Chicago when he was four years old, and five years later the father died leaving a widow and several small children without means of support. The son left school and worked in a chair factory to help support the family; then he engaged with Allen, Mack & Co., and advanced from errand boy to a more responsible place, when the firm failed. He began as messenger boy for the Western Union and worked up to the operating room, where he remained until he re signed to accept a place in the abstract department of the county, and during his six years' service he held almost every position in the recorder's office. Elected to the general assembly in '90

SAMUEL E. ERICKSON.

he energetically worked in the interests of his constituents. He is now a deputy under Sheriff Gilbert, who considers him one of the brightest and most trustworthy of his men. He has shown marked ability as a dramatic reader and is not married. Ten years ago he traveled extensively in Europe. In '92 was urged for congress: named for temporary speaker and declined.

Committees: Judicial department, municipal corporations, live stock and dairying, military, printing, drainage, world's fair.

THOMAS F. FERNS.

Ferns, Thomas F., (dem.), Jerseyville; lawyer. Born in Jerseyville July 27, 1862. Graduated from the Jerseyville high school in '82, and from the St. Louis Law School in June, '85, having been admitted to the bar March 20 previous. Mr. Ferns' success as a practitioner was pronounced from the start. He was city attorney of Jerseyville for three consecutive terms from '85 to '91, and was elected to the legislature in '90, and has a record that justifies his constituents, wisdom in sending him here. During the session of '91 he introduced and pushed to enactment a stringent law forbidding the organization of trusts and combinations to control markets and prevent open and fair competition. Although young he is one of the leaders in the house and has quite a reputation for ability and oratory. In past campaigns in western Illinois he has taken conspicuous part. He is already being urged for congress next year, and his record in the past justifies the opinion that he will get there.

JAMES P. FLETCHER.

Committees: Railroads (chairman), judiciary, judicial department, senatorial apportionment, education, finance, federal relations, steering committee.

Fletcher, James P., (rep.), Ridge Farm, Vermilion Co.; farmer. Born Feb. 14, 1855, almost on the spot where his house now stands, and was educated at Vermilion Academy and at Penn College, Oskaloosa, Iowa. Is married and has farmed all his life. He owns a fine herd of Chester White hogs, of which he is an extensive breeder. Is a Royal Arch Mason and has been worshipful master of his lodge for five terms; is also a Modern Woodman; is business manager of his lodge and was a delegate to the last state convention at Peoria. He is interested in any legislation that will benefit the farmers, particularly permanent roads. He has never held office before, and is in constant attendance.

Committees: Canal-river improvement and commerce, manufactures, public buildings, visit educational institutions, farm drainage, to investigate the Wann disaster

Farrell, James H., (dem.), Chicago; real estate. Born in the Isle of Jersey, Nov. 19, 1842; his father was born in the Isle of Guernsey, Victor Hugo's birthplace, and his mother in Dublin. All the schooling he had was obtained before he was 10 years old. He arrived in New York in '51, and began life as a clerk. When 19 he enlisted in Co. H of the famous 5th N. Y. Inf., Col. Judson Kilpatrick, commanding, and beginning with the battle of Big Bethel he was in nearly every important battle and skirmish of the Army of the Potomac during the war. When he was mustered out he entered the largest wall paper manufacturing concern in the union as clerk, and remained there until '68 when he moved to Chicago, continuing in the same line for two years. He has been in the real estate business for the past ten years. He has always taken great interest in politics, and is now serving his fourth consecutive term in the house. He organized and commanded the Cook County Democratic Marching club, the best drilled and most famous political marching organiza-

JAMES H. FARRELL.

tion in the country. He is also grand marshal of the democratic marching clubs for Illinois, having been elected in '84. He has been a leader in the house since his first election, and has served on all the most important committees, and while he does not push himself forward is regarded as a man of ability and influence. He is married and in independent circumstances.

Committees: World's fair (chairman—also chairman in the last legislature), judicial department, penal and reformatory, finance, municipal corporations, revenue, military, senatorial apportionment, steering com'ittee

DAVID FORSYTHE.

Forsythe, David, (dem.), Elwood, Will Co.; farmer. Born in County Antrim, Ireland, April 25, 1850, and in his eleventh year the family emigrated to America --an elder son and brother —the late John Forsythe, of Chicago, having preceded them by several years. David Forsythe resided with his brother in Chicago until he had completed his education in Chicago schools. He moved to Will county in '65 and has since been engaged in farming and shipping live stock, in which he has been very successful. He is married and owns 960 acres of land, gathered by his own industry and shrewdness. He has been supervisor of his township for three years, and has held minor offices. He was elected to the house in '90, re-elected in '92 and has served on important committees and taken an active interest in legislation each session.

Committees: Live stock and dairying (chairman), corporations, canal river improvement and commerce, mines and mining, agriculture, sanitary affairs, retrenchment, miscellaneous subjects.

Fowler, H. Robert, (dem.), Elizabethtown; lawyer, was born in Pope county about 35 years ago, and was educated in the common schools, finishing at the Northern Normal, graduating in '78. He taught school eight years; has been principal of the schools at Elizabethtown and Cave-in-Rock, and was very successful, raising the schools in Hardin county several degrees in efficiency. He graduated in law at Ann Arbor University in '85; was admitted to practice in Michigan in '84 and in Illinois in '85. He was states attorney of Hardin county for four years. Mr. Fowler has had to fight for every step of vantage ground since early boyhood, and in the face of almost unsurmountable obstacles has attained a place of influence and standing. He made a record for energy as chairman of the special committee to investigate the accident at Wann that commends him to his colleagues, who recognize his ability and honesty. He is championing a co-employe bill to protect railroad employes, and one introduced by himself to secure state uniformity of text books.

H. ROB'T FOWLER.

Committees: Judiciary, world's fair, election, fees and salaries, roads and bridges, revenue, visit educational institutions, county and township organization.

Goodall, Samuel H., (dem.), Marion; lawyer. Born in Marion Feb. 7, 1866, and graduated at the Southern Illinois Normal University in '87; taught school for two years in Williamson county and received a state certificate to teach. Graduated from the Ann Arbor Law School with the degree of L.L.B. in '90; was quiz master in the school in '90 and '91, and in this latter year received the degree of L.L.M. Was admited to the bar in Illinois in '90 and began practicing his profession next year, in which he has been successful. He has been city attorney of Marion and is not married. He is very anxious to cut down the usurous rates for tax sales, and get his county

into democratic congressional and senatorial districts. Is an aggressive and independent member with nerve enough to demand and insist that his section be given fair treatment.

SAMUEL H. GOODALL.

Committees: Miscellaneous subjects (chairman), judiciary, judicial department, education, mines and mining, claims.

Gleeson, James F., (dem.), Chicago; telegraph operator. Born in Chicago Jan. 17, 1859, and graduated in the commercial course of the Watertown (Wis.) branch of Notre Dame University. He had charge of the West Division police telegraph system as superintendent for over six years, and in '84 helped put up the first police boxes in the city. He was elected to

JAMES F. GLEESON.

the house in '86 and returned in '92. Is not married. He is a strong worker in the democratic party in Chicago, and Speaker Crafts has recognized his ability by placing him on several important committees. In the legislature of '87 he was active in the interest of labor legislation.

Committees: Municipal corporations, corporations, labor and industrial affairs, military affairs, printing.

Gill, Michael J., (dem.), Alton; glass-worker. Born in New York City Dec. 5, 1866, and is one of the promising young men of the house. His parents moved to Kentucky in '68 and he went to Alton in '82, where he has since resided, although he learned his trade in Wellington, O., in '81. His schooling was entirely at night, as he could not afford the time during the day; he learned German unaided. He is married, and already has made his influence felt in the house as a champion of the rights of the laboring classes. Is aggressive in their behalf.

MICHAEL J. GILL.

Committees: World's fair, mines and mining, labor and industrial, public buildings, fish and game, and others of less importance.

Gower, Bailey A., (rep.), Odell; farmer and stock raiser. Born in Franklin Co., Me., Oct. 27, 1835, and moved to Livingston Co., Ill., in '56, where he has lived and earned a standing and reputation second to none. His education was completed at the Maine Wesleyan Seminary, at Kent's Hill. He taught school for a time when a young man, but has farmed nearly all his life. He has filled various offices of minor importance. Is married and owns 950 acres of Livingston county land, and there is none better in the wide world. In the way of live stock he makes a specialty of road and carriage horses and thoroughbred cattle. He is regarded as one of the substantial and reliable men of the house. He has always voted the republican ticket, casting his first vote for Lincoln in '60. He is always in attendance when the house meets.

BAILEY A. GOWER.

Committees: Mines and mining, contingent expenses, fish and game, public buildings.

Griggs, Edward H., (rep.), Chicago; fire insurance. Born in Dedham, Mass., March 19, 1835. Came to Illinois in '56 and was educated in the common schools. He was clerk of what is now the Second National Bank of Rockford from '56 to '65. In '65 he bought an interest in The Rockford Register, which he ran successfully as a republican paper until 1874, when he

EDWARD H. GRIGGS.

relinquished it and moved to Chicago, where he has since resided. For the past ten years he has been connected with the western department of the

Niagara Fire Insurance company of New York. He was secretary of the senate in '71, and was a committee clerk in the senate of '69. Was elected to the house in '90, and kept tally for the republicans on the clerk of the house during the long and exciting contest for United States senator in '91. He is a quiet man, a hard worker in committee and a staunch republican. He is married.

Committees: Insurance, education, enrolled and engrossed bills, fish and game, senatorial apportionment.

Guffin, Washington I., (rep.), Paw Paw; grain and coal dealer. Born in Carlisle, N. Y., Jan. 17, 1840, and moved to Illinois in '69, settling on a farm near Mahigin's Grove, Lee county, where he went into the dairy and cheese industry. In '72 the Burlington railroad ran a branch through the county, and established the town of Compton, where Mr. Guffin built an elevator, also one at Paw Paw, and engaged in the grain business, with his home at Compton. Sixteen years later he moved to Paw Paw. He was educated in the common and select schools near his boyhood home, owns real estate in Paw Paw and Evanston, and is married. He was on the county board in '72; but never was on a jury, was a witness in court only once, and never had a case in court as plaintiff or defendant. He is very independ-

WASHINGTON I. GUFFIN.

ent in his utterance and a good legislator. He was nominated for the legislature by the Lee county convention by acclamation. Is always present.

Committees: Congressional apportionment, revenue, appropriations, municipal corporations, municipal and state indebtedness.

Guthrie, Noah H., (rep.), Aledo; farmer. Born in Green Co., Pa., March 6, 1842, and received a common school education. He worked on a farm until '61, when he answered the summons to arms, enlisting in Co. A, 7th W. Va. Inf., and served with credit for over three years. He was in all

NOAH H. GUTHRIE.

the great battles of the Army of the Potomac, and was wounded in the right leg at Spottsylvania, necessitating the removal of eight inches of the tibia. It is not apparent in his gait, and is regarded as one of the wonders of surgery. In Dec. '64, he came to Illinois and was appointed to the Illinois Soldiers' College at Fulton, remaining from '67 to '70. He took the U. S. census for his county in '70; was elected sheriff the same year, and re-elected in '72, and has farmed most of the time since. Is married and owns 280 acres of land, all finely improved. He took the census of his township in '80 and was elected to the house in '92.

Committees: Mines and mining, live stock and dairying, sanitary affairs, fish and game, contingent expenses.

Hanker, Charles, (rep.), Toledo; contractor and builder, was born in Wittenberg, Prussia, May 4, 1843, and moved with his father to America in '62 settling first in Freeburg, St. Clair Co., Ill., where he learned the carpenter trade. He moved to Cumberland county in '67 and engaged in the furniture business. He is married and owns considerable city property. He has held various minor offices and has been chairman of the republican county central committee. Opportunities for education were not as plentiful as now, and he received the common school education of the time in which he was a youth. He is a quiet and modest member but watches closely the moves of the leaders on the floor,

CHARLES HANKER.

and is faithful in attendance. He is a good, reliable representative.

Committees: Fees and salaries, public buildings, labor and industrial, manufactures, military.

Hanna, D. Caswell, (rep.), Monmouth; farmer and stock raiser. Born in Warren Co., June 8, 1836, and received a common school education. In '60 he went to Colorado and New Mexico, spending over a year mining, teaming, etc. He returned home and enlisted in

D. CASWELL HANNA.

Co. C 91st Ill. Inf., in Aug. '62; was elected first lieutenant. Saw his first service in Elizabethtown, Ky., where the rebel Gen. John Morgan captured

his command Dec. 25, '62. He remained in Benton barracks, Mo., on parole until June '63, when he was exchanged and sent to Vicksburg, arriving a few days after the surrender. After a scouting service of several weeks he reached New Orleans in August, was promoted to the command of his company, and participated in the principal battles of the Army of the Gulf, including Banks' campaign to Texas and the Rio Grande, winding up his service in Mobile after taking part in the siege of Spanish Fort and Fort Blakely. He was discharged July 27, '65 and returned home. Was married Oct. 17, '66 to Miss Martha E. Heaton, and has a family of five girls and four boys. He lived in Henderson county for many years and in '69 was elected county clerk, and re-elected in '73; was also mayor of Oquawka one term.

JAY L. HASTINGS.

In '76 he moved to Monmouth; is interested chiefly in agricultural and educational measures.

Committees: Worlds fair, license, farm drainage.

Hastings, Jay L., (rep.), Galesburg; lawyer. Born June 6, 1858, twelve miles north of Ottawa, Ill. His father is now a lumber merchant in Bay City, Mich. Mr. Hastings remained on the LaSalle county farm until he was 12 years old, when his parents moved on a Michigan farm. Afterwards he entered Lombard University, at Galesburg, maintaining himself by corresponding for Chicago, St. Louis papers and the Associated Press. He graduated in '76 and while in school earned a flattering reputation for ability and as an orator. He was on The Chicago Tribune for a time, and then entered the law office of Hon. O. F. Price, and in two years was admitted to the bar. He ear.y took great interest and became prominent in local and county politics. He was public administrator of Knox county for four years and has been alderman many years. Marr'ed.

Committees: Judiciary, municipal corporations, county and township organization, building and loan associations, elections.

Hawks, James A., (rep.), Atwood; grain and lumber dealer. Born in Oswego, N. Y., July 19, 1847, and educated at Falley Seminary, Fulton, N. Y., and Hamilton College, graduating in '69. He enlisted in the 3d N. Y. Art. when but 17 years old, and was captured and placed in Libby prison, from which place he was released when Gen. Grant captured Richmond. After the war he resumed his studies and moved to Piatt Co., Ill., in '69 and

JAMES A. HAWKS.

started in the general merchandise business. In '87 he branched off into grain and lumber, and has been dealing in these two ever since. He is married and owns 1,280 acres of land. He has been supervisor and held various minor offices. He was elected to the house in '82 and returned in '92, and no man stands higher among his colleagues. He has no hobbies, and scans closely every measure that comes up. He is a good legislator.

Committees: Banks and banking, finance, drainage, claims.

Hawley, Edgar C., (rep.), Dundee; merchant and stock raiser. Republican leader of the house. Born in Barrington, Ill., Feb. 20, 1850, and was educated in the public schools and Elgin Academy. Is married. Was cashier of the State Grain Inspector's office in Chicago for a time, and at present carries on a large business at Dundee. Was elected to the house of representatives in '88, '90, and '92. Was the republican caucus nominee

EDGAR C. HAWLEY.

for speaker in the present general assembly, and as such became the party leader and was conceded a chairmanship with clerk and room for use of republican members. He has taken an important part in the legislation of the general assemblies of which he has been a member; is a strong party man and a very shrewd politician.

Committees: Rights of the minority—the steering committee—(chairman), railroads, finance, penal and reformatory, banks and banking, agriculture, live stock and dairying, rules.

EDWARD J. HAYES.

Hayes, Edward J., (dem.), Chicago; merchant. Born in Ansonia, Conn., July 9, 1863, and moved to Chicago with his parents when four months old. He was educated in the public schools and worked in a stove foundry for ten years. The first public office he has held is the present one. Although one of the youngest members, Mr. Hayes has been complimented by places on several important committees. Is not married.

Committees: Municipal corporations, elections, revenue, license, retrenchment, executive department, labor and industrial affairs.

* Holtslaw, Daniel W., (dem.), Iuka; farmer. Born in Marion county, Feb. 5, 1849; educated in the county schools. Is married and owns 400 acres.

Committees: Visit educational institutions, (chairman), congressional apportionment, appropriations, mines and mining.

Henning, Edgar L., (dem.), Plano; banker and merchant. Born in Kendall county, April 8, 1849, and educated in the common schools, at a commercial college and Ann Arbor. He started in life on a farm, then began clerking in a store, and in '75 engaged in the mercantile line himself, continuing it up to the present day. He started E. L. Henning's Bank in '79, and it is one of the most substantial and safe institutions in the state. He is married, and owns 600 acres of land besides town and city property. He has held various local offices, and has been on the board of education for nine years, and president of the board for four. He is a very industrious

EDGAR L. HENNING.

member, and for his first session is well posted on legislative work. He is a good democrat and valuable member.

Committees: Executive department (chairman), banks and banking, appropriations, canal river improvement and commerce, agriculture, building and loan associations, state and municipal indebtedness.

Herdman, Alexander B., (dem.), Morrisonville; miller and grain dealer. Born in Orange Co., N. Y., Jan. 5, 1837, and moved to Illinois with his parents in '42, settling first in Randolph county, where he remained for 12 years; they he moved to Jersey county, remaining until '67; then to

ALEXANDER B. HERDMAN.

Brighton, where he remained until '71, and from '71 to the present time he has been a resident of Morrisonville and engaged in his present business. He always voted the democratic ticket. Was educated in the common school branches in public and select schools, and finished his education at Westminister College, Fulton, Mo. Is married and owns 160 acres in Jersey county. Has been connected with school offices all his life; has been on the board of supervisors for several years and was chairman one year and has been on town boards and president of the same. He desires very much to see democratic pledges of economy and reform fulfilled, and every time the opportunity occurs votes in that direction.

Committees: To visit state charitable institutions (chairman), appropriations, revenue, county and township organization, world's fair, canal and river improvement and commerce, state institutions.

Higgins, Richard T., (rep.), Vandalia; banker. Born in Cass county, Ill., June 9, 1842, and left an orphan at the age of 12. When 15 he left the farm to make his home with his brother-in-law, Dr. F. B. Haller, of Vandalia. He took a full academic course at Tuscarora Academy, Pa., and obtained a complete medical education at the Chicago Medical College, and Jefferson Medical College, Philadelphia. He entered the union service as a hospital steward and was promoted on his merits to be assistant surgeon. In '64 he returned home and entered into partnership with Dr.

RICHARD T. HIGGINS.

Haller. Although very successful in his profession he was compelled to abandon it to take care of his large business interests. In '75 he was elected president of the Farmers and Merchants National Bank, which place he now fills. He is married and owns 1,500 acres of farm land in addition to considerable city real estate. He has held various offices of minor importance; was nominated by acclamation.

Committees: Railroads, appropriations, worlds fair, sanitary affairs.

JOHN HOLMES.

Holmes, John, (dem.), Medina; farmer. Born in County Londonderry, Ireland, June 15, 1824, and emigrated to Canada with his parents in '27, stopping for a short time and moving on to New York, where the family remained for eight years. In '35 they located on a wild piece of land within a mile of Mr. Holmes' present home. He has farmed all his life, is healthy, vigorous, and owns 2,500 acres of magnificent land farming has paid under his careful guidance, energy and thrift. He is married and has a family of ten children, and if they carry their character in their faces as does their father, they can borrow all they want without making a note. He received an indifferent education in district schools. He is popular and respected by his neighbors or he would not have held office for 32 of the 35 years he has lived in Medina township since he was 21: he was postmaster seven years and member of the county board for five years, being chairman one term. Mr.

ARCHIBALD W. HOPKINS.

Holmes was too modest to permit the telling of how he saved Peoria county thousands of dollars in the building of the new court house in the 70's.

Committees: Canal and river improvement and commerce, public buildings, claims, agriculture, soldiers' home, horticulture.

Hopkins, Archibald W., (rep.), Granville, Putnam Co.; farmer. Born 1½ miles east of Granville, and has lived on the same spot ever since, his father having settled there fifty-eight years ago. He was educated in the public schools and at Hillsdale College, Mich. Is not married. Hon. Joel W. Hopkins, his father, was a republican member of the 27th General Assembly, and is 79 years old. They own and operate a great deal of valuable land in Putnam and Bureau counties. Mr. Hopkins declined to give the number of acres. He has a record as a legislator that will bear the closest scrutiny, and is one of the hardest workers in the house. In '78 he spent five months traveling in Europe, and has visited about every point of interest in the west and a great deal of the south. He was elected to the house in '90 and '92.

Committees: Appropriations, sanitary affairs, military, to visit educational institutions, worlds fair.

Johnson, Caleb C., (dem.), Sterling; lawyer. Born on a farm in Whiteside county May 23, 1844. Educated in the common schools and spent a term in the military academy at Fulton. Admitted to practice law in '67 and began practice in '69. Was in the army as a member of Co. C, 69th Illinois, and Co. D, 140th Illinois. Whiteside county is overwhelmingly republican, and the opportunities for preferment of a

CALEB C. JOHNSON.

democrat are few and far between; has been a member of the board of supervisors, and was deputy collector of internal revenue during Cleveland's administration. He was a delegate to the national democratic convention in '88. In '85 and '87 was a member of the house and was one of the democratic leaders. It was the session of '85 that Col. Morrison and Gen. Logan fought for the U. S. senatorship, and Mr. Johnson was a firm friend of the Waterloo statesman. Is married.

Committees: Judicial department and practice (chairman), rules, steering committee, municipal corporations, federal relations, miscellaneous subjects, joint committee on enrolled and engrossed bills, congressional apportionment, county and township organization.

Jones, Alba M., (rep.), Milford; merchant. Born in Stockland township, Iroquois Co., May 23, 1856, and was educated in the common schools with finishing touches at Valparaiso University. Is married and well-to-do in this world's goods. He has been a

ALBA M. JONES.

member of the board of supervisors for seven years, and on the board of education for five years, and was chairman of the board in '90-'91. Has no hobbies or fancies to work off during the session, but favors any legislation that is beneficial to the people of the state. Is present at every session and is a good representative.

Committees: World's fair, roads and bridges, building and loan associations, military, farm drainage, senatorial apportionment.

NORMAN L. JONES.

Jones, Norman L., (dem.), Carrollton; abstracts and loans. Born in Patterson, Ill., Sept. 19, 1870, and is the "baby" of the general assembly.

His father moved his family to Carrollton in '72 and here Mr. Jones was educated in the high school, graduating in '88, and completing his studies at Valparaiso and West Point Military Academy. He taught school for two winters in Fayette, Ill. Is not married, and has not been a voter long enough to have a record as a servant of the people. Although it is early in the session he gives promise of becoming a useful and influential member, and is a credit to his constituents, his party and himself.

Committees: Judicial department, appropriations, education, military, executive department, manufactures, library.

*Johnson, Richard M., (rep), Levings; farmer. Born in Morgan Co., Ky., Feb. 24, 1842; educated in common schools and served in the Union army in Co. A, 22d Ky. Inf. Is married and owns 200 acres.

Committees: Warehouses, world's fair, federal relations, miscellaneous.

Kaiser, Louis, (rep.), Bushnell; retired merchant. Born in Vacha, Kingdom of Saxony, July 29, 1841, and in '58 emigrated alone when 17 years old to Burlington, Iowa, where he remained until April, '61, when he started in business for himself in the dry goods line at Young America, now Kirkwood, Ill. He remained there until '65, when he moved to Bushnell continuing the same business until '91, when he

LOUIS KAISER.

retired to enjoy the accumulations of thirty years' close application to business. He went into business for himself at 19, was married at 21, and a grandfather at 45; is possessed of an independent fortune, including 1,600 acres of land, the fruit of hard work and shrewdness. He has been mayor of Bushnell for three terms, one term on the board of education, and president of the Bushnell fair for several years. He received a common school education, and is bending his energies toward securing a uniform text book law for Illinois, and also advocates a

LAWRENCE KELLY.

law that permits the payment of taxes semi-annually, to benefit the farmer.

Committees: Appropriations, finance, warehouses, horticulture, elections.

Kelly, Lawrence, (dem.), Martinsville; farmer. Born in County Westmeath, Ireland, Dec. 15, 1837, and on the death of his father his mother started with him for the new world in '48, but she died on the ocean. He landed in New Orleans friendless and alone and drifted around until '50, when he settled in Clark Co., Ill., in the same school district that is now his home. Mr. Kelly has had only a fair education. Is comfortable so far as this world's goods go, having accumulated over 200 acres of fertile land by industry, frugality and close attention to business. His main characteristic is a sturdy spirit of self-reliance. Is married. He has represented his township in the county board, and was elected to the house in '90 and '92. In the session of '91 he stood in the front rank for Palmer for U. S. senator; is a conservative and careful member, and is very popular among his colleagues.

Committees: Contingent expenses (chairman), live stock and dairying, agriculture, railroads, horticulture, state institutions, roads and bridges, executive department, retrenchment.

King, William H., (rep.), Chicago; real estate and loans. Born in Erie Co., N. Y., Feb. 25, 1844, and moved to Chicago in Aug. '68, and has lived there ever since. He practically educated himself in the common school branches. President Lincoln's call for troops in '61 aroused his patriotism

WILLIAM H. KING.

and he responded by enlisting in Co. B, 14th Wis. Inf., in June, '61, and served for nearly four years, participating in the battles of Fort Donelson, Shiloh (where he was wounded in the head and left leg), Corinth, Iuka, Jackson, Vicksburg (where he was wounded in the right arm), the Red River expedition, and was in the campaign from Nashville to Savannah with Sherman. He received five gunshot wounds. Is married. Learned the carpenter's trade before the war. He is a 32d degree Mason, and past post commander of the G. A. R., and has also been treasurer of the Veteran Union League for the past eight years.

Committees: Municipal corporations, penal and reformatory, insurance, fish and game, executive department.

*Kroh, Philip H., (dem.), Anna; preacher. Born in Frederick Co., Va., Feb. 10, 1824; educated at Woodward College, Cincinnati, and at the Columbus Theological Seminary; was chaplain of the 109th Ill. Inf. Elected county superintendent of schools in '63; is married.

Committees: History (chairman), public charities, public buildings, manufactures, claims, roads and bridges.

Kent, William E., (rep.), Chicago; real estate. Born in County Cork, Ireland, Jan. 6, 1861, and emigrated with his parents to Middletown, Conn., in '64. He was educated in the common schools of Connecticut, working on the farm meantime. He moved to Chicago in '81; learned the carpenter's trade and followed it for two years. Then he went into the Custom House as clerk under Jesse Spaulding, remaining for another two years, and was deputy coroner of Cook county for four years. He studied civil engineering and took contracts for sinking mines and erecting shaftings, and other work in that connection. He was in this line when he lost his eyesight in Feb. '92, a man who was crazy drunk blazing away at him with both barrels of a shot-gun. To the surprise of everyone he recovered, but lost both eyes. Since then he has dabbled in real estate to some extent. He has always been very active in republican politics, and is one of the shrewdest republican workers in Cook county. He was delegate to national republican conventions in '84 and '88, and alternate-at-large in '92; has been on the Cook county committee for many years off and on. He was a member of the house in '89.

Committees: Corporations, municipal corporations, warehouses, license, retrenchment.

Kwasigroch, John A., (dem.), Chicago; real estate. Born in Polish Germany Jan. 18, 1866—was the second

WILLIAM E. KENT.

youngest member of the 37th general assembly, and was re-elected to the present legislature by an increased majority. Moved to Chicago in '71 and educated in the St. Stanislaus Kostka parish school. After the death of his father was employed as messenger by the American District Telegraph company, and is now engaged in the real estate business. He was one of the "101" who stood by Gen. Palmer from start to finish without flinching in '91,

JOHN A. KWASIGROCH.

and had several important committee assignments. Is very prominent in Cook county politics; is not married.

Committees: Corporations, warehouses, sanitary affairs, printing, miscellaneous subjects, license, world's fair.

Langhenry, Godfred, (rep.), Chicago; lawyer. Born in Chicago April 1, 1861, and has lived in the metropolis all his life. Was educated in the common schools, and at the age of 15 went into the wholesale house of Marshall

GODFRED LANGHENRY.

Field & Co., where he remained until he was 29, being promoted from stock boy to charge of a section of the notion department. During the last two years he was there he attended evening classes in the Chicago College of Law, graduated in June, '90, and immediately began practicing his profession, devoting himself exclusively to civil business, and has had more than ordinary success. He is also secretary-treasurer of the Eagle Lithographing Co., one of the largest concerns in Chicago; is married.

Committees: Railroads, judiciary, municipal corporations, executive department, libraries, steering committee.

Leavitt, Thomas N., (rep.), Maroa; merchant and banker. Born in Rockingham county, N. H., October 6, 1838, and moved to Peoria with his parents in '44, and to Maroa in '61, rented a farm and settled down. The call for troops aroused his martial ardor and he enlisted in Co. C, 66th Ill. Inf., and after three years' hard service he

THOMAS N. LEAVITT.

returned to the plow and sickle. After two years' farm work he started a grocery store in Maroa, and gradually added farm implements and other lines; then went into the lumber and coal business, and in '91 assisted in organizing the State Bank of Clinton, of which he is president; is also president of the Leavitt & Oglevee Co., dealers in farm implements and lumber. For a few months he was a fireman on the first railroad that ran into Peoria the present Peoria division of the Rock Island. He was educated in the public schools and finished at the Northern Illinois institute, then a thriving institution at Henry. Is married, and besides bank stock, etc., and real estate, owns 1,000 acres of land; was postmaster of Maroa for 17 years, and has been supervisor and chairman of the Macon county board.

Committees: Revenue, warehouses, banks and banking, manufactures, miscellaneous.

*Lewis, Albert W., (rep.), Harrisburg; lawyer. Born Nov. 30, 1856, in Clinton Co., O. Educated at Wilmington (O.) College and was admitted to the bar in '82. Is married, and has held minor offices—city attorney, state's attorney, etc.

Committees: Judicial department, fees and salaries, building and loan associations, congressional apportionment.

Lyman, William H., (dem.), Chicago; contractor. Born in Chicago June 27, 1861, and was educated in the public schools of that city. He afterwards traveled four years for M. Shields & Co. Is married. He is now a partner with his father as a contractor, and they do a large and profitable business. He was elected to the general assembly in '88, '90, and was returned in '92 by an increased majority. In the session of '91 he participated in the stirring scenes incident to the election of Gen. Palmer to the U. S. Senate, and risked his life for many days in order to cast his vote in the joint assembly, having been carried into the house in an invalid's chair. He pays particular attention to the wants of the laboring man, and

WILLIAM H. LYMAN.

in '91 had charge in the house of the bill to prevent non-union cigar factories using union labels or imitations thereof, which became a law.

Committees: Municipal corporations (chairman), railroads, fees and salaries, labor and industrial affairs, libraries, congressional apportionment.

McGee, J. Park, (dem.), Tuscola; physician and stock raiser. Born in Clark Co., Ind., Jan. 5, 1848, and moved to Douglas county in '74 and has been there ever since. He was educated in the public schools and at Wabash college. His medical education was obtained in Cincinnati. Rush

J. PARK M'GEE.

Medical College conferred a complimentary degree on him for services rendered the medical profession in the legislative session of '85. When only 16 years of age he enlisted in the army as a private in Co. K, 137th Ind. Inf. Is not married, owns 350 acres of land, and is extensively engaged in raising trotting horses. He has been nominated to the house three times—every year that Cleveland ran for president found Dr. McGee on the democratic ticket for representative—and he was elected every time, and served on the appropriations committee each session.

Committees: Building and loan associations (chairman), appropriations, education, warehouses, finance, to visit penal and reformatory institutions.

*McClure, Samuel H., (dem.), Eureka; farmer. Born in Danville, Ill., Nov. 2, 1827; educated in common schools; was in the mercantile business fourteen years. Is married, and owns 800 acres. He has held various township offices.

Committees: County and township organization, public charities, roads and bridges, farm drainage, horticulture.

McGinley, James E., (dem.), Chicago; plumber. Born in Chicago March 6, 1866, and educated at a Catholic parochial school and the West Division High School, graduating from the latter. He learned his father's trade; is a member of the firm of J. McGinley & Sons, plumbers. He is a young man with a bright political future before him. Was one of the first to be elected on the ward commit-

JAMES E. M'GINLEY.

tee under the new constitution of the Cook County Democracy. Is not married. Was elected to the house by a labor constituency, and pays especial attention to their wants; he also advocates any legislation that will compel the railroads to elevate their tracks in Chicago, and has a bill in the house which will accomplish that result.

Committees: Corporations, license, sanitry affairs, libraries, retrenchment.

McInerney, Michael, (dem.), Chicago; manufacturer. Born in Ireland

MICHAEL M'INERNEY.

Feb. 2, 1857, and moved to Chicago when 14 years old. Received a common school education and has always been known as one of the working democrats of Cook county. He amassed a fortune by shrewd operations in real estate, and is secretary-treasurer of one of the largest brick manufactories in the state. He has been collector of the Town of Lake. Is married. He was elected to the house in '90 and re-elected in '92. In the first session he took an active interest in the election of Gen. Palmer to the senate, and contributed not a little to the general's success. Mr. McInerney has been a leader in both sessions.

Committees: Enrolled and engrossed bills (chairman), warehouses, corporations, penal and reformatory institutions, municipal corporations, banks and banking, live stock and dairying, loan and homestead associations, senatorial apportionment, steering committee.

McKinlay, Robert L., (dem.), Paris; lawyer. The democratic leader in the

ROBERT L. M'KINLAY.

house. Born in Cincinnati July 14, 1839, and moved to Paris in '68. He was educated in the common schools of Cincinnati, graduating in the high school, and spent some time at the Annapolis naval academy. Obtained his legal education at the Cincinnati Law School, graduating in '61, being admitted to the bar the same year. He was captain of Co. A, 59th, and adjutant of the 22d O. Inf.; saw hard service in West Virginia and west Tennessee. Returning from the army he took up the practice of his profession, and is regarded as one of the most successful lawyers in Eastern Illinois. Is married and owns considerable property in Paris. He was city attorney of Paris for many years, and was elected to the house in '76, '78, '86 and '92. He made a magnificent canvass of the state in '84, as democratic candidate for attorney-general, and ran a hopeless race against J. G. Cannon for congress in '88. He is one of the strongest men in the house, and as chairman of the committee on appropriations has charge of that important subject in the house.

Committees: Appropriations (chairman), steering committee (chairman), rules, judiciary, municipal corporations, joint rules, education, finance, federal relations, county and township organization.

*McCrone, George C., (rep.), Quincy; lawyer. Born near Hartford, Conn., Aug. 22, 1857, and spent two years as a western cattle herder; educated at Dartmouth College and Ann Arbor. Elected to the house in '90 and '92. Is married.

Committees: Judiciary, municipal corporations, claims, retrenchment.

*McMurdy, Robert, (rep.), Chicago; lawyer. Born in Frankfort, Ky., March 8, 1860, and received a collegiate education. Is married.

Committees: Judiciary, municipal corporations, elections, congressional apportionment, world's fair.

McKenzie, John C., (rep.), Elizabeth; lawyer. Born in Woodbine township, Jo Daviess Co., Feb. 18, 1860. He received a common school education and studied law with Judge W. T. Hodson, of Galena, and was admitted to practice in '89. He worked on a farm when not at school in his youth. He

JOHN C. M'KENZIE.

has practiced his profession since '89 and is also interested in the shipping of live stock, in which he is extensively engaged. He has been supervisor and has held various minor offices. Is married and is in comfortable circumstances. Mr. McKenzie is not a silent member of the house. Nor does he make many speeches—he fills a mean between the two extremes.

Committees: Roads and bridges, insurance, fish and game, miscellaneous subjects, judicial department, printing.

McKnight, Sargeant, (rep.), Girard; real estate. Born in Macoupin Co.,

SARGEANT M'KNIGHT.

Ill., Jan. 6, 1844; parents were Virginians. He was educated in common schools, and enlisted as a private in Co. H., 122d Ill. Inf. in Aug., '62. Was elected first sergeant and promoted to second lieutenant Dec. 31, '62. Served as inspector on the staff of Col. Hicks, commanding post of Paducah, Ky., and participated in the repulse of Gen. Forrest on Fort Anderson in March, '64. Later he served as provost marshal of the city of Paducah. In Dec. '64, he was appointed aide-de-camp on the staff of Gen. Garrard, commanding second division, 16th army corps, and participated in the battle of Nashville Dec. 15-16, '64. Promoted to captain by brevet by the president "for gallant and meritorious services during the campaign against the city of Mobile and defenses"; was mustered out of service in July, '65, and returned to Girard, engaging in the dry goods business and the manufacture of woolen goods, and remained in active business until '89. In May, '66, was married to Miss Virginia A. Boggen. Served as member of the board of supervisors of Macoupin county; for four years was captain in the 5th regiment, I. N. G.; was aide-de-camp on the staff of Gov. Fifer with rank of colonel. He is past commander of Luke Mayfield post, G. A. R., and was representative from Illinois to the national encampment at

Boston; in '93 was again selected—as a delegate-at-large to the national encampment. Was aide-de-camp on the staff of Gens. Veazey and Palmer, commanders-in-chief, G. A. R. He was chosen minority candidate for representative from the 38th district without opposition.

Committees Steering committee, railroads, county and township organization, live stoc s and dairying, claims, retrenchment, senatorial apportionment.

McMillan, James T., (dem.), Jacksonville; lawyer. Born on a farm near Springfield Jan. 27, 1840, and when 13 years old his father moved on a farm near Jacksonville, permitting Mr. McMillan to attend the Jacksonville schools. He graduated from the high school while Hon. Newton Bateman was principal. Then he spent three years in Illinois College and one year in the literary department of Ann Arbor University. He graduated from Union College, New York, in '63, and took a term of medicine at Columbia College and eight months at Bellevue Hospital. He was one of a number who volunteered to go to the battle field of Antietam and care for the sick and wounded, but the labor was too arduous and he had to give it up. Still thirsting for the highest medical education, he returned to Ann Arbor for another term and graduated in medicine. But he discovered that he could

JAMES T. M'MILLAN.

not stand the night work and hard life of a physician, so he quit it and took up the law, and after graduating at Ann Arbor located in Detroit, remaining about a year, and then he returned to Jacksonville, where he has been ever since. He gives a great deal of atten-

tion to 600 acres of land owned by his wife and himself. He is married and a member of the grange organization.

Committees: Judiciary, judicial department, elections, banks and banking, public buildings, roads and bridges.

Martin, John S., (rep.), Bridgeport; teacher. Born Oct. 29, 1861, on a Law-

JOHN S. MARTIN.

rence county farm, and educated in the common schools. Attended the Central Normal College of Indiana, paying his tuition by teaching. This illustrates the character of the man, full of pluck and energy. Never held an office before and did not seek the present place in the house. Is married. He is a strong advocate of compulsory education and is decidedly in favor of state uniformity of text books. Mr. Martin is always present and is a useful and able legislator.

Committees: Education, printing, libraries, history-geology and science, fish and game, state and municipal indebtedness.

Merritt, Edward L., (dem.), Springfield; journalist. Was born in New York City. While yet a child his parents moved to a farm near Lebanon, Ill. Schools were of a poor quality then, and he only attended one for twelve months, being apprenticed in the printing business at the age of 11. The family removing to Salem, the father started The Advocate, Edward L. going with him, and becoming a good practical printer. For about four years he was civil engineer on the O. & M. R. R. In '58 he bought an interest in The Salem Advocate, and edited it until '65, when he bought an interest in The Springfield Register. He was identified with this paper for fifteen years as editor and publisher, and made a great reputation for the paper and himself throughout the union. He was a member of the state committee for twelve years at this time, and was secretary for several campaigns. In '74 and '76 he was practically the manager of the democratic campaign. He has always been in advance of his party on the tariff, being practically a free trader, taking that position in the state convention of '71, and succeeding after a hard fight in having a plank adopted that was clear and emphatic. In '66 President Johnson appointed him pension agent at Springfield, but the senate rejected him on account of his political views; he was reappointed twice and rejected each time. He was elected to the house in '90 and again in '92, and was a leader and on the steering committee

a bill giving the laboring people a Saturday half-holiday, which failed of passage through no fault of Mr. May. He is very active in important legislation and closely watches measures per-

STEPHEN D. MAY.

taining to the interests of his constituents.

Committees: License (chairman), judiciary, judicial department, finance, building and loan associations, insurance, contingent expenses, congressional apportionment.

Meyer, Charles F., (rep.), Kirkland; farmer. Born in Hanover, Germany, Jan. 1, 1843, and in '60 emigrated to the New World, coming direct to the garden spot, northern Illinois. Enlisted in Co. A, 153d Ill. Inf. He

EDWARD L. MERRITT.

in each. His family is one of the most prominent in the state in politics, journalism and war. Is married.

Committees: Insurance (chairman), education, appropriations, military, world's fair, agriculture, sen.torial apportionment, penal and reformatory, steering committee.

May, Stephen D., (dem.), Chicago; lawyer. Born in Belvidere, Ill., June 3, 1861, and educated at Illinois College, Jacksonville, and Ann Arbor, graduating from the latter in '84. He was admitted to practice in '86 and has attained a commanding position at the Chicago bar. He is not married. He was elected to the house in '90 from a strong republican district and was returned last fall. Mr. May was one of Gov. Palmer's staunchest friends during the memorable senatorial contest of '91, and in the same session introduced and championed with energy

CHARLES F. MEYER.

taught school at various points in northern Illinois for several years, and in '67 commenced farming, is at it yet and has made it pay, for he owns 345 acres of splendid land in DeKalb county. Is married and has held several town and school offices. Mr. Meyer is a quiet member, but posts himself on every measure that comes up and votes intelligently.

Committees: Revenue, public charities, mines and mining, congressional apportionment.

Meyer, Ernst, (dem.), Deer Plain, Calhoun Co.; farmer. Born Nov. 26, 1831, in Prussia, and received his education at the Berlin High School. He came to the United States in '60 and worked as a laborer on the Delaware & Lackawanna railroad; also on a farm. In June, '62, he enlisted in the Army of the Potomac, and served until the close of the war. He participated in the battles of the Wilderness, Spottsylvania, Cold Harbor and Petersburg. Was wounded at Ream's Station, Va., and limps in conse-

educated in the common schools and at the Christian Brothers University, St. Louis, graduating in '59. He has always been a farmer, is married and owns 250 acres of splendid land. He

JOSEPH E. MILLER.

was a member of the county board for two terms and has held various minor offices. He inaugurated his work in the house by defeating the aim of a number of the older members, who sought to kill the dairy commissioner bill, which is in the interest of the farmer and dairyman. He is particularly strong in committee work.

Committees: Fees and salaries, live stock and dairying, drainage, fish and game, soldiers' home, world's fair, horticulture.

ERNST MEYER.

quence. He never applied for a pension. He moved to Calhoun Co., Ill., in July, '65, and engaged in farming. He was county commissioner four years, and as a school director had his district adopt the system of providing the school children with necessary text books free. As a member of the house in '91 he helped elect Senator Palmer, and on no roll call was he "absent or not voting." In May, '76, he married Miss Amelia Dinkler, has three sons and lives on his extensive farm of 2,800 acres at Deer Plain.

Committees: soldiers' home (chairman), canal-river improvement and commerce, education, military, drainage, fish and game, horticulture.

Miller, Joseph E., (dem.), Belleville; farmer and stock raiser, was born in St. Clair county June 8, 1842. He was

JOHN MEYER.

Meyer, John, (rep.), Chicago; lawyer. Born in the Kingdom of Holland Feb. 27, 1852, emigrated to Chicago in '67 and has lived there ever since. Received his education at the Northwestern University and the Union College of Law, graduating in '79; was admitted to the bar the same year, and has had a very successful practice every since, almost exclusively in civil cases. Is married and was elected to the house in '86, '88, '92. He is one of the republican leaders in the present house; is a quick, forcible speaker and a splendid parliamentarian. In the session of '89 he handled the measure creating the Chicago Sanitary District for drainage purposes, and to his skillful generalship is attributed to a great extent the success of the measure.

Committees: Judiciary, corporations, insurance, elections, senatorial apportionment, steering committee.

Mitchell, Benjamin Marion, (dem.), Chicago; printer and publisher. Born in Quincy Jan. 30, 1869. When he was seven months old his parents moved to Chicago, and he was educated in the public schools of that city, graduating from the Brown school on the West Side. Is a member of the Cook County Democratic, the Chicago Bachelors and County Democracy Marching clubs. He has worked for the Western Union, for Marshall Field, Schlesinger & Mayer and Pardridge; was chief bundle wrapper in Coutant & Co.'s, filled the same position and was promoted timekeeper in

BENJAMIN M. MITCHELL.

the Bee-Hive. Then he was general city agent for the Cable Cigar Co. He was elected at 19 secretary of the regular Thirteenth Ward Democratic Club, which he held until '90, when he was made president of the club, and has taken an active part in all campaigns. Is not married. Lives at 75 Columbia place, near Garfield Park, and is a good speaker.

Committees: Municipal corporations, revenue, warehouses, fees and salaries, building and loan associations, military, miscellaneous, printing.

Moore, William A., (dem.), Morton; farmer. Born in Todd Co., Ky., Nov.

WILLIAM A. MOORE.

1, 1839, and when but seven years old his parents moved to Illinois and settled in Woodford county, near the present site of Eureka. There he spent his youth and obtained an education, the opportunities for which in that early day were exceedingly limited. However, pluck and energy with sufficient ambition to attract spurred him on, and by hard knocks he learned the common school branches. He worked in daylight and studied by the light of a tallow dip. At the age of 19 he obtained a certificate to teach. In '62 he married, and in '63 moved to Morton township, where he now resides on his farm; he owns 400 acres of as good land as the sun ever shone upon. He has always been a stalwart democrat, and has been honored with many minor offices, and was a member of the house in '77, declining a unanimous renomination in '78 on account of sickness in his family. He is one of the best representatives of the agricultural class in the general assembly and his former experience has been of value to him this session. The interests of the agriculturist are carefully guarded by him. Mr. Moore is always in his seat during sessions.

Committees: Horticulture (chairman), canal-river improvement and commerce, penal and reformatory, state institutions, revenue, federal relations, claims, drainage.

Morris, Freeman P., (dem.), Watseka; lawyer. Born in Cook county, March 19, 1854, and when 20 years old moved to Watseka. He received his education in Chicago and his legal education at the Union Law College; was admitted to the bar in '74. Is married, and owns a handsome home with splendid appointments in Watseka besides other valuable real estate. April 21, '93, Gov. Altgeld appointed Mr. Morris on his staff with the rank of colonel. He has held various local offices and was elected to the house in '84, '88 and '92, and has had a great deal to do in moulding legislation at every session. He is one of the best lawyers in this session, so prolific in great legal minds, and possesses an easy, graceful delivery in speaking that is pleasing and effective. Is chairman broken, and insisted on the house ordering an investigation of the state auditor's and state treasurer's offices, carrying the point against very influential members - republican and dem-

WILLIAM L. MOUNTS.

ocratic. He believes all interest should be covered into the treasury.

Committees: State and municipal indebtedness (chairman), municipal corporations, judiciary, insurance, state institutions, fees and salaries, military, federal relations.

Muir, Robert H., (rep.). Clyde, Cook Co.; clerk. Born in Glasgow, Scotland, April 17, 1848, and emigrated with his parents to America in '50, stopping first at Syracuse; then in turn his father moved to Quebec, Stratford and Naponee, Canada,

FREE. P. MORRIS.

of the caucus, is one of the democratic leaders and is on the steering committee.

Committees: Judiciary (chairman), judicial department, municipal corporations, insurance, license, world's fair, federal relations, rules, joint rules, enrolled and engrossed bills, steering committee.

Mounts, William L., (dem.), Carlinville; lawyer and banker, was born in Carlinville Aug. 31, 1862, and educated at Blackburn University, graduating in the scientific course. Is married and owns and controls 2,000 acres of farm and coal land. He has held the offices of city treasurer, city attorney and is the present mayor of Carlinville. He was secretary of the democratic committee of Macoupin county for eight years, and stands high in the estimation of his constituents. He believes that pledges are not made by politicians and parties to be

ROBERT H. MUIR.

finally settling in Chicago in '66. He received a good education in the common schools and at Naponee University, graduating in '65; he also graduated from the Union College of Law, Chicago, in '79, and was admitted to practice in '81. He did not practice long, however. He has been trustee of the town of Cicero, president of the school board and school trustee, and has been a deputy clerk in the Cook county circuit clerk's office fourteen years, a place which he now fills to the satisfaction of those with whom he comes in contact. He is a careful and painstaking legislator, and examines all measures that come up. Is married.

Committees: Senatorial apportionment, license, warehouses, labor and industrial affairs, agriculture, judicial department.

Mulligan, Joseph H., (dem.), Kewanee; railroad agent. Born in Kentucky Sept. 12, 1855, and a year later his parents moved to Young America, afterwards Kirkwood, Ill., where he received what education he has in the public schools. Is married and began life as a farm hand, quitting this to work as laborer on the present Rock Island branch of the Burlington road; then he worked on a section for several years, and got a job switching in the Biggsville yards in '73. Here he picked up telegraphy and was made night operator at Biggsville in '76; promoted to be agent four years later, transferred to Kirkwood, and finally settled in the Kewanee office of the Burlington in '85. It is one of the most important

JOSEPH H. MULLIGAN.

offices on the road in Illinois, standing about sixth in volume of business done. He strongly advocates a uniform text book bill, is always present and votes intelligently on all measures.

Committees: Retrenchment (chairman), corporations, building and loan associations, labor and industrial affairs, mines and mining, world's fair.

Murdoch, Frank, (rep.), Oneida; banker. Born in Ayrshire, Scotland, Sept. 2, 1843, and came to America in '52 with his parents, stopping first in Trumbull Co., O. Moved to Knox Co., Ill., in '57, and settled on a farm near

FRANK MURDOCH.

Oneida. He was educated in the common schools and farmed until '73, when he went into the banking business and has been in it ever since. The Exchange Bank of Oneida is owned by Anderson & Murdoch. He is highly regarded by his neighbors, for they elected him alderman for eight years and mayor for four years, and he has been a member of the school board for six or seven years; was chairman of the republican county committee for two years. Is married. He is a 32d degree Mason; been master of his lodge for eight or ten years; High Priest of the chapter; Past Commander of Galesburg Commandery No. 8, K. T., and a Past Grand in the Odd Fellows.

Committees: Banks and banking, finance, insurance, live stock and dairying, military affairs.

Murphy, Joseph L., (dem.), Pinckneyville; grain dealer. Born on a Perry county farm, Dec. 31, 1840, and educated in the public schools. Is married and owns about 600 acres of land. He began life in the mercantile business, and afterwards dealt in lumber and grain. He finally dropped the lumber business and added real estate and has been very successful in it as well as in his grain business. He has been mayor of Pinckneyville for the past fifteen or sixteen years and is mayor at this time. In September, '62, he enlisted in Co. D, 110th Ill. Inf., and most of his fighting was done in Palmer's Fourteenth Corps. He was in the campaign before Atlanta and

JOSEPH L. MURPHY.

the march to the sea of Sherman's legions. He went in as a private and came out a captain, being promoted for gallant conduct. He has no pet schemes to foster, but is anxious to do his share towards the general good of the people. Mr. Murphy is one of the most reliable representatives.

Committees: Federal relations (chairman), revenue, railroads, penal and reformatory, public charities, state and municipal indebtedness, senatorial apportionment.

GEORGE MURRAY.

Murray, George, (rep.), Elmira, Stark Co.; farmer. Born in Rexburyshire, Scotland, May 1, 1840, and moved to America with his parents in '53, coming direct to Stark county, and has been there ever since. He received a common school education and is married. He began farm work when 14 years old and has been on a farm ever since, and owns over 800 acres of Stark county land. He has held several township and school offices, and is a typical farmer. He is willing that the democrats shall have free swing to institute the "reforms" they have insisted were necessary. Mr. Murray is always in his seat and informs himself as to the merits of all bills.

Committees: Canal-river improvement and commerce, labor and industrial affairs, drainage, horticulture.

Myers, William H., (dem.), Terre Haute, Henderson Co.; blacksmithfarmer. Born in Jennings Co., Ind., Feb. 28, 1849. The family moved first to Lewis Co., Mo., thence to Terre Haute, Ill. At the age of 7 years he met with an accident that crippled

WILLIAM H. MYERS.

him for life, but with indomitable energy and a pluck that has been a characteristic of his life, he proceeded to carve out a future. He was educated in the common schools and is in independent circumstances. He was elected to the house in '90 and reelected in '92, running ahead of his ticket each time, and no man in Henderson county is more popular. He is a good servant of the people and his two terms in the house have demonstrated the fact that no mistake was made in his election.

Committees: Agriculture (chairman), corporations, live stock and dairying, labor and industrial, drainage, contingent expenses, farm drainage, congressional apportionment.

Noling, Lars M., (rep.), Rockford; real estate. Born in Sweden May 4, 1843, and emigrated to Rockford in '64. Common school education. Married.
Committees: History, manufactures, federal relations, horticulture.

Nohe, Augustus W., (rep.), Chicago; broker. Born in Baden, Germany, Nov. 27, 1846, and came to this country in '51. He settled In Freeport, where he remained until '75, when he moved to Chicago. He received a common school education and is married. He was elected to the house in '90 and returned in '92 by an increased majority. He has represented his ward in the Chicago city council. During the war he was connected with the military telegraph and did valuable service for the union armies. He was with Gen.

AUGUSTUS W. NOHE.

Schofield for a time and joined Sherman at Goldsboro, N. C., finishing his field service at Raleigh. The government required his aid after the war, however, and he was sent to Nashville, Tenn., where he remained on duty for Uncle Sam until '67, when he was mustered out of the volunteer service, being probably the last war telegrapher to retire. Then he engaged in the same profession in Chicago, and is now in the brokerage business. He is one of the most forcible and aggressive members of the house, and is endeavoring to pass his bill removing the $5,000 limit for damages for death by railroad accidents. He also strongly favors municipal control of gas and electric lighting plants, and has a bill before the house that will accomplish that object.
Committees: Corporations, municipal corporations, banks and banking, building and loan associations, congressional apportion.

O'Connell, Edmund, (rep.), Bloomington; lawyer. Born in Franklin Co., N. Y., Nov. 20, 1848. Educated in the district schools and at Franklin Academy, Malone, N. Y., and coming

EDMUND O'CONNELL.

to Illinois in '71 he taught school and studied law until '74, when he was admitted to the bar. He began the practice of his profession in Bloomington, where he settled in '73, and is regarded as one of the best lawyers in Central Illinois, being particularly strong as a jury pleader. He is a leader in the present house, as he was in the last general assembly; is strong in debate, an eloquent, forcible speaker; married.
Committees: Corporations, education, building and homestead associations, elections, license, steering committee.

EDWARD J. NOVAK.

Novak, Edward J., (dem.), Chicago; real estate. Born in Chicago Nov. 2, 1869, and with probably one exception is the youngest member of the general assembly. He was educated in the public schools and at the Metropole Business College, graduating from the latter. He entered the office of the county treasurer of Cook county when George R. Davis was treasurer and has been there ever since, the office now being in charge of Charles Kern. He is an energetic worker in Cook county politics. This is the first office to which he has been elected, but if he keeps up the record he has made thus far it will not be his last. Is not married. Is interested in measures that will benefit the laboring people.

Committees: Manufactures (chairman), appropriations, insurance, sanitary affairs, world's fair, libraries, history-geology and science.

O'Connor, James, (dem.), Chicago; professor of music, was born in Libertyville, Lake Co., Illinois, Oct. 2, 1848, and was educated at the district schools. When 19 years old he went to Chicago and learned the trade of mechanical engineer. Afterwards he moved to Louisiana and worked at his trade there. In '73 Gov. Wm. Pitt Kellogg appointed him justice of the peace for St. Bernard's Parish, a suburb of New Orleans. In '74 while hunting he lost his sight by an unfortunate accident and has been totally blind ever since. Terrible as is such an affliction he did not lose courage,

JAMES O'CONNOR.

but battled against the world with more persistency than ever. He returned to Chicago and took up the profession of music, which he has followed ever since. Through his talents and intelligence there has been opened up to the blind an entirely new field. He is the only blind man in the world that has successfully lead an orchestra and done his own prompting. His especial mission here is to have the legislature reappropriate the $100,000 he succeeded in getting from the legislature of '87 to establish in Chicago an Industrial Home for the Blind. This bill he got

JOSEPH A. O'DONNELL.

through the session of '87, of which he was a member, but Gov. Oglesby failed to appoint a board of trustees and the money lapsed into the treasury. He is a man of talent and ability outside his profession, and takes an active part in all legislation. He succeeded in securing from the city council of Chicago last year an appropriation of $50,000 to establish a Mental and Manual Training School for the blind. He is married.

Committees: Public charities, appropriations, corporations, license, manufactures, history-geology and science.

O'Donnell, Joseph A., (dem.), Chicago; lawyer. Born in Ballina, County Mayo, Ireland, Dec. 23, 1860. Educated in the public schools and began the battle of life on his own account when 11 years old as an employe in a machine shop, and was promoted to a foremanship when 20 years old. Meantime he studied law, perfected himself in his studies, was admitted to the bar in '87 and began practice in Chicago, where he has been very successful. He was elected to the house in '88, '90, '92, and is one of the most eloquent defenders of the rights of the common people in the general assembly. Is married.

Committees: Elections (chairman), judiciary, corporations, congressional apportionment, steering committee, loan and homestead associations, and others.

O'Loughlin, Michael, (dem.), Seneca; farmer. Born in County Clare, Ireland, Nov. 18, 1845. Emigrated to Wisconsin with his parents in '49, and to LaSalle Co., Ill., in '66. He was educated in the public schools of Wisconsin and taught district school in Illinois for five years. Is married and owns 640 acres of land. He was a supervisor for twelve years and school treasurer for his township for ten years. He is one of the quiet, substantial men of the house, and closely watches legislation, particularly that which pertains to agriculture and the Illinois river valley. He was one of the most reliable members of the last house, as he is of the present. As one of the "101" who elected Palmer senator, Mr. O'Loughlin never faltered.

Committees: Canal-river improvement and commerce (chairman), live stock and

MICHAEL O'LOUGHLIN.

dairying, revenue, railroads, agriculture, county and township organization, insurance, farm drainage.

Paddock, Daniel H., (rep.), Kankakee; lawyer. One of the republican leaders in the house, was born in Lockport, Ill., April 5, 1852; is a son of Col. John W. Paddock, and of ancestry on both sides that runs back to the Plymouth colony. Educated in Illinois' public schools and at the Albany Law School, graduating in '74, and admitted to the bar the same year in Illinois. His home has been in Kankakee since Nov. 6, '53, where his father was a practicing lawyer. Mr. Paddock is prominent in republican politics in the state, and a man of influence and high standing. After two terms as states attorney for Kankakee county, he was elected to the legislature in '88, and returned in '90 and '92. Is one of the ablest parliamentarians and probably the best debater on the republican side. Is married. Mr. Paddock has been a leader in the three last legislatures.

DANIEL H. PADDOCK.

Committees: Judiciary, railroads, penal and reformatory, education, insurance, rules, steering committee.

Painter, Oscar, (rep.), Metamora; stock raiser and farmer. Born in Northumberland, Pa., March 10, 1846, and moved with his parents to Woodford Co., Ill., in '48, and has been there ever since. Ten years of his life were spent teaching school, and the balance farming and stock raising. He was educated in the common schools and is not married. He stands high where

OSCAR PAINTER.

he is best known, for in a race for the shrievality once he ran several hundred ahead of his ticket, although the overwhelming democratic majority was too much to overcome. He pays particular attention to the needs of the farmer, and makes a good representative. He is in comfortable circumstances.

Committees: Canal-river improvement and commerce, public charities, public buildings, federal relations.

Payne, William, (rep.), Osborn: farmer. Born in Scott Co., Iowa, March 4, 1841, and lived on a farm for the first ten years of his life and then moved with his parents to Hampton, Ill. Was educated in the public schools, and at 18 taught school, leaving that occupation to shoulder a musket to battle for his country, enlisting in the 13th Ill. Inf., the first 3-year regiment in the service. For four years he escaped the bullets of the enemy and returned to Illinois, spending a year in a commercial college, and then

WILLIAM PAYNE.

entered the county treasurer's office, Rock Island. From '66 to '70 he was deputy sheriff, and was sheriff from '70 to '74, and in '74 he moved on a farm in Zuma township and has been there ever since, as farmer, breeder and shipper of stock. Is married, and owns 540 acres. Elected to the house in '91 to fill vacancy caused by the ineligibility of W. F. Collins, he was re-elected in '92, having been re-nominated by acclamation. He is one of the most reliable and best members.

Committees: Canal-river improvement and commerce, revenue, federal relations, retrenchment, roads and bridges, farm drainage.

Parrott, Walter S., (dem.) Litchfield; journalist. Born in Raymond, Montgomery Co., Ill., May 4, 1865, and is one of the youngest members in the house. He was educated at Blackburn University and at the Northern Indiana Normal at Valparaiso. Is married. Has had considerable experience on the country press, and published a paper at Raymond for several

WALTER S. PARROTT.

years. He lived in Raymond for 25 years, and got every democratic vote cast in that township. Although young, Mr. Parrott has already familiarized himself with the technicalities of legislative life, and his farmer constituents have no cause to apologize for his youth, nor will it be necessary to excuse his votes.

Committees: To visit penal and reformatory institutions (chairman), congressional apportionment, senatorial apportionment, building and loan associations, manufactures, roads and bridges, printing.

BERNARD P. PRESTON.

Preston, Bernard P., (dem.), Littleton, Schuyler Co.; farmer. Born at Ithica, N. Y., March 27, 1838, and came to Illinois with his parents in '52. His education, which commenced on the site of Cornell University, was completed at St. Louis, after which he returned to the Schuyler county farm. He has a large farm, and raises the best breeds of horses and cattle. Is a good representative of the farming class in the legislature, advocates measures in their interest, and is always in his seat. Is married. Was elected to the house in '90 and again in '92, and has taken an active part in all important legislation

Committees: Farm drainage (chairman), penal and reformatory, state institutions, revenue, banks and banking, agriculture, live stock and dairying.

*Ramey, Thomas T., (rep.), Brooks; farmer. Born in Caldwell Co., Ky., March 6, 1823, and was educated in district schools. Is married and owns 200 acres; was elected to the house in '72, '88 and '92.

Ramsey, Charles A., (rep.), Hillsboro; retired merchant. Was born near Lewistown, Pa., Jan. 8, 1845, and was educated in the common schools with a short academic course. In Aug., '62, when only 17 years old, he left school and enlisted in Co. D, 148th Penn. Inf.; was appointed sergeant-major, and afterwards promoted to adjutant of the regiment. After three years of hard service he was mustered

CHARLES A. RAMSEY.

out and moved to Shelby Co., Ill., where he remained two years and then moved to Irving, Montgomery county, where he engaged in the drug business until '77. Then he went to Hillsboro and engaged in the hardware and agricultural implement lines until Jan., '92, when he disposed of his stock. He was made president of the Hillsboro National Bank when it was organized in '82 and is still at the head of it. He never was an office-seeker, but was elected three times to the county board and was chairman for one term. He is present mayor of Hillsboro. Is married and owns 700 acres of land.

Committees: Revenue, contingent expenses, mines and mining, fish and game.

GEORGE REED.

Reed, George, (rep.), Belvidere; farmer. Born in Westfield, Mass., May 26, 1824, and moved to Illinois in '47, stopping in Boone county. Afterwards he moved to Winnebago county, remaining there for two years and then returned to Boone. He was educated in the common and district schools of his youth, gaining more by his own efforts than through teachers. He has farmed all his life, and is a good exemplification of what can be accomplished by pluck, sagacity and industry, for he owns 525 acres of as good land as the sun ever shone upon. Illustrative of the difficulties under which he labored it may be said that he patented 120 acres from the government and had to borrow the money to pay for it, paying 50 per cent. for the loan. He is married and credits his wife with much of his success. He has held nearly every township office and was supervisor for twelve years, and was chairman of the board several times; has been on the county agricultural board 25 years and president of it for 8 years; was a member of the state board of agriculture for two terms; was elected to the house in '90 and re-elected in '92. He is interested in two creameries that manufacture a quarter of a million pounds of butter annually. Is director in the Peoples bank of

Belvidere. He is always in attendance during sessions. A good legislator.

Committees: Appropriations, roads and bridges, county and township organization, live stock and dairying, miscellaneous subjects.

Rohrer, Louis, (dem.). Somonauk: farmer. Born in Alsace-Lorraine, France, Jan. 6, 1837, and emigrated with his parents in '45, coming to La-Salle county. He was educated in the common schools. Has never been an officeholder to any extent and never sought an office. He has been on the county board of La Salle county and was elected to the house in '90 and returned in '92. Is married and owns over 800 acres of fine land. He is anxious to see some of the reforms promised by the democratic state convention carried out, and especially is he in favor of the enactment of a uniform text-book law.

LOUIS ROHRER.

Committees: Drainage (chairman), canal river improvement and commerce, fish and game, live stock and dairying, warehouses, agriculture.

Rottger, Frederick W., (dem.), Mt. Sterling; lumber and grain merchant. Born near Menden, Prussia, Aug. 8, 1844, and emigrated with his father in '50, coming via New Orleans. They took a boat up the Mississippi and Illinois rivers to Naples, thence by the old Naples & Jacksonville strap railroad to Jacksonville. After remaining in Jacksonville two years he was bound out to E. S. Hinrichsen, who owned a farm seven miles east of town. Mr. Hinrichsen afterwards moved to Alexander and was made agent of the Great Western railroad, now the Wabash, and Fred. was office boy. He was finally promoted to take complete charge of the station, and in '65 was sent to Mt. Sterling to take charge of that office. He has held it ever since. He gradually became involved in farming and added lumber

FREDERICK W. ROTTGER.

and grain buying and horse buying and selling. He was successful at everything he touched, and is now well off. He is married and owns 945 acres of land. Never an office seeker he has been mayor of Mt. Sterling and on the county board. He educated himself.

Committees: Appropriations, fees and salaries, roads and bridges, county and township organization, claims, charitable institutions.

Seawell, Charles W., (dem.), Greenville; mercantile business. Born on a

CHARLES W. SEAWELL.

farm in Washington Co., Ill., Oct. 19, 1853, and received his education in the district schools. He was raised on a farm and his early manhood was spent in the hard work of a farmer. Afterwards he went into the mercantile business, wholesale and retail, at which he was very successful. He is one of the hardest workers and shrewdest politicians in Illinois, and was a member of the house in '87. During that session, as well as the present one, he took an active part in all legislation, and was on some of the most important committees. Is married. He is strong in his political views, and has always been a democrat.

Committees: State institutions (chairman), senatorial apportionment, corporations, mines and mining, warehouses, military, contingent expenses.

Smith, James A., (dem.), Chatsworth; editor. Born in Vermilion, O., Aug. 6, 1845, and came to Illinois with his father a year later. He owns The Chatsworth Plaindealer, one of the best country newspapers in northern Illinois. Mr. Smith received a good

JAMES A. SMITH.

common school education. Was elected to the house in '88 and '90. In both sessions his ability as a leader was recognized and his advice sought. He works quietly but effectively. Is a strong party man and believes in strong party organization. Was married, but lost his wife two years ago.

Committees: Congressional apportionment (chairman), education, public charities, banks and banking, county and township organization, insurance, contingent expenses, enrolled and engrossed bills, license, steering committee.

Smith, Washington S., (dem.), Mt. Zion; farmer. Born in Bath Co., Ky., Sept. 27, 1850, and came with his parents to Illinois in '57, settling in Macon county, where Mr. Smith has resided ever since. He has filled various township offices, and was supervisor for six years, and was chairman of the board for two years, resigning in '90 to enter the house. Is married and owns and operates a fine farm. He is

WASHINGTON S. SMITH.

a strong democrat, and in advance of his party on economic questions. He was elected to the house with a democratic colleague in '90, and both were re-elected in '92, a sufficient evidence that the services of both were appreciated.

Committees: Fish and game (chairman), mines and mining, penal and reformatory, agriculture, labor and industrial affairs, farm drainage.

Snedeker, Orville A., (rep.), Jerseyville; real estate and lawyer. Born

ORVILLE A. SNEDEKER.

in Jerseyville June 11, 1848, and educated in the public schools of the county, such as they were at that time and at Shurtleff College; also a term at a commercial college. He was admitted to the bar in '71. Is married and has two boys, Isaac and Frank. He owns valuable real estate and farming lands. This is the first elective office ever held by him. He has frequently been nominated by conventions but declined to accept; his nomination last year for the house was the third time – he declined on two former occasions. The district from which he was elected included Jersey, Green and Scott counties - the 37th.

Committees: Worlds fair, agriculture, finance, printing, public charities and others of less importance.

Snyder, William H., (dem.). Belleville; lawyer. Born in Belleville June 29, 1858, and the third generation that has filled a legislative office in Illinois, his grandfather, Adam W. Snyder, being a member of the state senate in '35, and his father, the late Judge Wm. H. Snyder, being a member of the house in '51. He was educated in the public schools of Belleville and at Washington University, St. Louis. He read law with Hay & Knispel, Belleville, was admitted to the bar in '82 and began practicing his profession shortly afterwards. He has been city attorney of Belleville, and is not married. As a member of the special committee to investigate the accident at Wann he took an active and leading

WILLIAM H. SNYDER.

part, and also as a member of the elections committee.

Committees: Libraries (chairman), judiciary, judicial department, elections, penal and reformatory, history, Wann investigation (special).

Sparks, Thomas J., (dem.). Bushnell; lawyer. Born in Clinton Co.,

Ind., Aug. 16, 1843, and moved with his father to Illinois in '45, coming direct to Fulton county. He spent his youth on the farm and at 20 went to Lombard University, Galesburg, and afterwards to Howe's Academy, Mt. Pleasant, Iowa, graduating from the latter in '69. He then taught school

THOMAS J. SPARKS.

for eight years, reading law in the meantime. Was admitted to the bar in Nebraska in '71, and after practicing in that state for six years came to Illinois settling in Bushnell where he has lived ever since, and has built up a good practice. Is married and owns 240 acres of land. His recent eulogy in the house, of Justice Scholfield of the supreme court, attracted attention to his oratorical powers and his hard work in committees and on the floor has given him the reputation of being one of the ablest members of this general assembly.

Committees: Fees and salaries (chairman), judiciary, judicial department, railroads, education, senatorial apportionment, to visit penal and reformatory institutions.

Spellman, Thomas L., (rep.). Danville, also office in Owings Building, Chicago; mine operator. Born in Logan Co., O., Oct. 12, 1849. Leaving home at the age of 18 he learned telegraphy and was a railroad operator for several years. In '72 he married the daughter of William Tennery, one of the oldest and best known citizens of Vermillion county. He settled in Danville in '80 and has been very successful in business. He is a Mason of high degree, an Odd-Fellow, a Pythian, a Modern Woodman, a member of the Royal Arcanum and of the Mystic Shrine. Educated in the public schools.

Elected to the house in '90, and again in '92. Is a good member, and although a coal operator, was willing to concede to miners legislation to which they were justly entitled. He is a

THOMAS L. SPELLMAN.

staunch republican and believes in a strong party organization in the house.
Committees: Railroads, penal and reformatory, municipal corporations, claims.

*Straight, Rufus C., (rep.), Fairbury; farmer. Born on a farm in Chautauqua Co., N. Y., June 28, 1835; came to Illinois in '54; was a member of the school board for 25 years; is married; owns 1,500 acres. Member in '91 also.
Committees: Canal-river improvement and commerce, penal and reformatory, public charities, soldiers' home, agriculture.

LAWRENCE B. STRINGER.

Stringer, Lawrence B., (dem.), Lincoln; editor. Born in South Amboy, N. J., Feb. 24, 1866. He moved to Illinois with his parents in '76, and graduated in '82 at Gitting's Seminary, La-Harpe, and in '84 went to Lincoln, entering the college there, graduating in the classical course in '87. Then he acted as city editor of The Lincoln Times, and studied law. He frequently represented his college in oratorical contests; and in '88 stumped the state for the democratic ticket, winning new laurels as an orator and debater. He was of republican antecedents, but joined the democracy on the tariff issue in '88. Was elected to the house in '90 and again in '92 by an increased majority. Mr. Stringer was the youngest member of the legislature of '91. He takes prominent part in all important legislation, is popular with his colleagues, and his friends predict a brilliant future for him. Is married.
Committees: Education (chairman), mines and mining, labor and industrial affairs, elections, history, printing.

EDWARD STUBBLEFIELD.

Stubblefield, Edward, (rep.), McLean; farmer. Born in McLean county Aug. 15, 1834, and received a limited education, principally by absorption in contact with the world. He has farmed all his life. The Stubblefield family is inter-married with the Funks, another great McLean county family, Edward Stubblefield's mother being a Funk. The Stubblefields came from Virginia, Edward's father moving from Virginia to Ohio and thence to Illinois in '24. He has held various township offices, is married and owns over 800 acres of McLean county land, as valuable as any in the wide world. Mr. Stubblefield has always been a strong republican. He is regarded as a good, substantial farmer legislator.
Committees: Agriculture, drainage, horticulture, soldiers home.

Taggart, Captain T., (dem.), Cisne; physician, was born in Brown Co., Ind., Dec. 28, 1846, moved to Cisne in '86. He was educated in the common schools and received a first-class medical education at the Indianapolis Medical College, graduating in '79, although he took a first course of lecture in '74. When he became convinced that a real live war was upon the country he offered his services, enlisting June '61 in Co. G., 55th Ind. Inf., when he was not yet 15 years old, and remained until the close of the war, participating in the battles of Richmond, Perryville, Murfreesboro, Chattanooga, Missionary Ridge and the Georgia campaign. He was wounded twice—at Richmond in Aug. '62 his left leg was broken and in March '65 at Kingston, N. C., he was shot through the left arm. Is married and has held

CAPTAIN T. TAGGART.

various minor offices. He is a strong advocate of an economical government.

Committees: Public buildings and grounds (chairman), state institutions, penal and reformatory, soldiers home, education, sanitary affairs, history-geology and science.

Talbot, Prescott H., (rep.), Lindenwood, farmer. Was born in Killingly, Windham Co., Conn., Dec. 17, 1842, of parents who were descendants of the Puritans. In '62 he enlisted in Co. G, 74th Ill. Inf., and fought like a true patriot until the close of the war. He was severely wounded in '63 and had a hard fight for life, but was assisted by a strong and wiry constitution and an indomitable will. When his country needed him no longer he returned home and went to Rockford to complete his education, which had been interrupted by the war. Then he settled in Lynnville, Ogle Co., on a bleak prairie, which under his skillful handiwork soon bloomed with fruit of the soil. His energy, perseverance and thrift have enabled him to accumulate a com-

PRESCOTT H. TALBOT.

petency, for he he owns 331 acres of splendid Ogle county land. Although not seeking preferment, he has been honored many times by his neighbors with minor offices, and served for three years on the county board of supervisors. He was elected to the house in '90 and rendered valuable assistance to the farmers in legislative matters. Is married. He is one of the most valuable members.

Committees: Appropriations, military affairs, license, soldiers home.

HOMER J. TICE.

Tice, Homer J., (rep.), Greenview; farmer. Born in Menard county, Feb. 5, 1862. Educated at Lincoln University, graduating in the scientific course in '82 and also took a course in a business college in Bloomington. Was married and made a tour of Europe in '83 returning to his splendid farm of 500 acres near Greenview. Was nominated for the house in '90 on the 96th ballot and elected the same year, and was returned in '92. He is particularly active in the interest of the farmers. He is interested in the improvement of the Illinois river and after a hard fight got resolutions through the house with that object in view. Mr. Tice is one of the most reliable and ablest representatives the republicans of his district ever sent to Springfield.

Committees: Appropriations, penal and reformatory, agriculture, labor and industrial affairs, horticulture.

Wallace, William H., (rep.), Humbolt; farmer. Born in Ripley Co., Ind., Oct. 11, 1840, and moved to Coles Co., Ill., in '74. Educated in the common schools and at a commercial college and graduated in medicine at the Ohio Medical College, Cincinnati, in '67. After practicing his profession for nine years he turned his attention to farming, with flattering results. In the fall of '61 he enlisted in Co. F, 37th Ind. Inf., and served as a private, corporal, company clerk, regimental postmaster, assistant division postmaster, and division postmaster. The last two years of his service were in Louis-

WILLIAM H. WALLACE.

ville, where he had charge of the distribution of the military mail, a responsible and arduous position. He is married and owns over 860 acres of land. He was elected supervisor from his township by a majority of 19, although the township is democratic by 100, evidencing that he is best liked where he is best known. He is a faithful representative, always in his seat.

Committees: Live stock and dairying, state institutions, executive department, warehouses.

Warder, Walter, (rep.), Cairo; lawyer. Born at Maysville, Ky., April 7,

WALTER WARDER.

1851, his father moving to Johnson Co., Ill., next year. He was raised on a farm and participated in the hardships of a farmer boy in the 60's. He attended the public schools and completed his education at Illinois University, Champaign. Returning home he worked on the farm, taught school and studied law, applying himself industriously, and was admitted to the bar in Sept. '74, and immediatly began practice at Marion. In '76 he married Miss Dora Bain, daughter of John Bain, of Vienna, one of the wealthiest and most prominent citizens of Southern Illinois. In '80 he removed to Cairo. In '83 he was appointed states attorney of Alexander county to fill a vacancy; in '85 he was appointed master in chancery and has held the office ever since. Although of southern birth and democratic antecedents he has always been a republican, and is regarded as one of the strongest men in "Egypt." He has earned the reputation of being a conscientious and industrious member. He was the caucus nominee for temporary speaker last January; served on the leading committees of the session of '91, including the steering committee, and was re-elected by an increased vote in '92.

Committees: Judiciary, mines and mining, banks and banking, insurance, roads and bridges, congressional apportionment, steering committee.

*Thiemann, William, (rep.), Itasca; farmer. Born in Hanover, Germany, Feb. 11, 1849, and in '57 emigrated with his parents to DuPage county. He was elected to the house in '90 and '92; common school education. Is married and owns 290 acres.
Committees: Corporations, education, public charities, live stock and dairying, claims.

*Warren, James P., (dem.). Rose Hill, Jasper Co.; farmer, was born in Bartholomew Co., Ind., Sept. 25, 1842; in '52 the family settled in Jasper county; common school education; is married and owns 420 acres. Enlisted in Co. D, 97th Ill. Inf., and served three years.
Committees: Congressional apportionment, farm drainage, public buildings, state institutions.

Watson, James H., (dem.), Woodlawn, Jefferson Co.; physician. Born in Mt. Vernon July 31, 1846, and received a common school education. In '62 enlisted in Co. E, 70th Ill. Inf. After his discharge he was in the U. S. secret service under Gen. Palmer until the surrender of Lee. Then he studied medicine and graduated from the College of Physicians and Surgeons, St. Louis, and has successfully practiced his profession ever since. He has been supervisor, trustee of Woodlawn several times and for six years was on the board of pension ex-

JAMES H. WATSON.

aminers at Mt. Vernon. He has been delegate to conventions without number and was chairman of the senatorial committee of his district for four years. He was elected to the house in '90 and and again in '92, and in a quiet, unostentatious way acts well the part of a legislator. His investigation of abuses in the Anna insane asylum last session created a sensation.
Committees: Public charities (chairman), railroads, elections, military affairs, retrenchment, sanitary affairs, senatorial apportionment.

Wheelock, William W., (rep.), Chicago; lawyer. Born in Felts Mills,

WILLIAM W. WHEELOCK.

Jefferson Co., N. Y., Sept. 24, 1864, and educated at St. Lawrence University, Canton, N. Y., and at the Northwestern University Law School, Chicago. Moved to Chicago in '86, was admitted to the bar in '89, and was in Corporation Counsel Miller's office for a number of years, but is now practicing alone, and is very successful. Is not married. He was assistant attorney for the Chicago Drainage Board up to Jan. 1, '93, when he resigned to take his seat in the House. Chicago has three republican clubs for the three divisions of the city the Lincoln, the Hamilton and the Marquette clubs. He was the founder of the first, has been its secretary since it was organized and his shrewdness and ability in political matters is conceded. He is anxious to secure an amendment to the constitution that will permit the abolishment of the justice courts in Cook county, and the substitution therefor of district courts, and is heartily backed by the Supreme Court, the Chicago judges and the Chicago Bar association, and has good show of success.
Committees: Judiciary, judicial department, drainage, state institutions, military affairs, roads and bridges

*Weckler, Frederick S., (rep.), Fayetteville; farmer. Born in Peru, Ind., Sept. 10, 1848, and moved to Fayette-

ville in '69; educated at Notre Dame. Lost his wife three years ago, and owns 420 acres. Is justice of the peace.

Committees: Agriculture, mines and mining, labor and industrial affairs, license.

Whitley, Langley St. A., (dem.), Springfield; physician. Born in Springfield July 21, 1863, and educated in the public schools. Educated in the medical profession at St. Louis, at the College of Physicians and Surgeons, New York, at the Long Island Medical College in Brooklyn, and began to practice his profession in Springfield in '83, and was very successful. Is married and is interested in real estate. Is very strong with labor organizations and champions their cause in the house. He was a page in the house in '75, and has been chief surgeon of the Wabash railroad, middle division, in charge of

LANGLEY ST. A. WHITLEY.

their large hospital in Springfield, and has a great reputation for saving limbs when amputation seems almost a necessity.

Committees: Finance (chairman), appropriations, fish and game, public buildings, revenue, railroads, agriculture, congressional apportionment, mines and mining.

Wilkening, Conrad, (dem.), Crete; merchant. Born in Crete March 24, 1856, and educated at parochial and public schools and at Bryant & Strattan's Business College, Chicago, graduating when only 17 years of age. He has been engaged in the mercantile business for 23 years, and is the senior member of the firm of C. Wilkening & Co. They deal in general merchandise with a banking attachment. It is not only the largest department store in Crete, but the largest in Will county.

He never sought office in his life; has been school treasurer for ten or twelve years, and was nominated for the house against his protest. He lived in Chicago for a time. He is married and in

CONRAD WILKENING.

comfortable circumstances. He was interested in the repeal of the Edwards law and favors the enactment of another compulsory law with the objectionable features removed. He is quiet and accommodating and has made many friends.

Committees: Education, penal and reformatory, banks and banking, printing, libraries, world's fair.

Wilson, H. Clay, (rep.), Springfield; lawyer. Born in Davis Co., Ky., July 2, 1856, and on the outbreak of the

H. CLAY WILSON.

civil war his father removed with his family to Enterprise, Ind., in which state Mr. Wilson resided until '82, when he came to Sangamon Co., Ill.

At the age of 12 he began working on his father's farm and continued at it until he was 20, when he started to school at Danville, Ind., and graduated in the teacher's and commercial course. Then he came to Sangamon county and taught in the public schools for seven years, in the meantime studying law and was admitted to the bar in '88. Was nominated by the republicans for county judge in '90, but the overwhelming democratic majority was too much to overcome. He was unanimously nominated for the legislature in the spring of '92. Is married and has two interesting children. He takes great interest in fraternal and beneficiary societies, being a Mason, an Odd Fellow, a K. of P., an Elk, a Maccabee and a Modern Woodman. He is very popular and stands well with his colleagues.

Committees: Judicial department, corporations, labor and industrial affairs, building and loan associations, congressional apportionment, printing, penal and reformatory.

Wilson, James P., (dem.), Woosung; farmer. Born in Blair Co., Pa., June 7, 1854, and in '56 moved with his parents to Dixon, Ill. After attending Knox College, Galesburg, he taught school, and in '77 moved to Woosung, the heart of an agricultural paradise, where he has become a successful farmer, owning 160 acres of as good

JAMES P. WILSON.

land as the rain ever pattered on. He was a member of the Ogle county board of supervisors for many years and its chairman for one year. He was a member of the House in '77 and again in '91. As chairman of the committee on appropriations last session he made a record that will serve as an example for future leaders in a fight for an economical government. He is an orator of no mean ability as those who listened to his speech in Rochelle in '90 in presenting Gen. Palmer with a cane can testify, yet he seldom airs his eloquence in the house.

JACOB ZIMMERMAN.

Committees Revenue (chairman), agriculture, finance, live stock and dairying, elections, contingent expenses, senatorial apportionment, steering committee.

Zimmerman, Jacob, (dem.), Mount Carmel; farmer. Born on a farm near Greensburg, Pa., Sept. 27, 1831, and nine years later moved with his father's family to Stark Co., O., where they remained for three years, when they went to Upper Sandusky, and from there he moved to Marshall, Ill., in '52. Here in connection with the late James C. Robinson he established and published The Eastern Illinoisan, a paper of wide circulation and influence in democratic circles in that day. It was here in '53 that he introduced the plan of a primary election instead of delegate conventions for nominating county officers; he was the pioneer in this innovation which was necessary in that early day on account of the trading and combinations of candidates. He ran The Eastern Illinoisan for four years and then moved to Urbana, where he established The Constitution, a democratic paper, of course, which he ran for four years, through the panic of '57; was legislative correspondent for The State Register in '57. In '60 he moved to Mt. Carmel and established The Democrat, which ran during the campaign as a red hot Douglas champion. After the election he abandoned journalism for the farm except occasional contributions to the press. He was a successful tobacco farmer for many years, but now farms in a general way including live stock. While at Marshall he bought two printing offices; one was used in establishing The Eastern Illinoisan and the other was taken to Greenup to start The Cumberland County Democrat; it was the first paper that county had. He was educated in the common and select schools, is married and owns abut 350 acres of land. He has been on the county board and held minor offices, and was elected to the house in '78. He is anxious to see this legislature amend the revenue law by changing the time for taking final judgment against delinquent taxpayers to July, so that farmers can realize on their crops before their taxes are collected. He is on more important committees than any other member.

Committees: County and township organization (chairman), rules, appropriations, revenue, judicial department, roads and bridges, drainage, federal relations, horticulture.

*Wilke, Fred, (rep.) Beecher; farmer. Born in Westphalia, Germany, March 17, 1829, and emigrated to Will county in '60. Common school education; is married; elected to the house in '88, '90 and '92. He has been supervisor since '71.

Committees: Canal-river improvement and commerce, penal and reformatory, roads and bridges, drainage.

*Wiwi, Philip, (dem.), Montrose; merchant. Born in Rhenish Bavaria, June 10, 1833, and emigrated to Indiana in '50; moved to Illinois in '67; educated in common schools; elected to the house in '90 and '92. Is married and owns 1,100 acres.

Committees: Claims (chairman), public charities, public buildings, elections, soldiers' home.

In the "make-up" it was necessary to change a few of the biographical sketches from their true alphabetical position. An effort was made to get every portrait in its place—in the biography, or immediately preceding it. It is no fault of the compiler and publisher that the House of Representatives is not represented by a complete portrait gallery. Poverty on the part of those whose sketches are marked with a * is no good reason, for without exception, almost, the biography indicates a degree of prosperity above the average citizen and legislator.

THE PRESS GALLERY.

Some of the brightest stars in the journalistic firmament have sent us as "hot stuff" from Springfield as they ever will send in this world. The writer's experience as a legislative correspondent dates from the session of '83, when the little unpleasantness over Mr. Rook and the passage of the Harper High License Bill, furnished gingery sensations for weeks. The next legislature—that of '85—contained 101 democrats and E. M. Haines and 102 republicans, and the correspondents wanted plenty of space. Guns, knives, clubs and grim death were only ordinary diurnal incidents of both sessions until the points at issue were finally adjusted. The meetings in '87 and '89 were comparatively peaceful, but '91 was hot enough. No ordinary material could cope with the events of these sessions of the Illinois General Assembly, and the managing editors appreciated the gravity of the assignment by detailing their best men. Among others who have burned the wires the following are noted: R. W. Ransom, now night editor of The Tribune; V. B. Kelly, lately of The New York Sun; Charles M. Pepper, now chief of the Washington staff of The Chicago Tribune; Walter Wellman, now chief of the Washington staff of The Chicago Herald; John F. Ballantyne, afterwards managing editor of The Chicago Herald and Daily News; Charles R. Tuttle, now managing editor of The Chicago Dispatch; Phocion Howard was an omnipresent and indispensable adjunct—peace to his weary bones; Brand Whitlock, now chief clerk of the index department of the Secretary of State's office; Dan Ambrose, now running a paper in Missouri; L. W. Busby, now assistant editor on The Inter Ocean; E. L. Merritt, now a representative in the house from Sangamon county; Will Connelly, now owner of the Danville Daily Press, and others whose names are not now recalled. John A. Corwin, on duty in '81-3 for The Times, switched to The Herald, and finally landed with The Tribune; is now in charge of that journal's legislative bureau, and has had it for several sessions. Mr. Corwin is the oldest correspondent in consecutive service with the Illinois General Assembly. T. C. MacMillan, now in charge of the The Inter Ocean staff, was a member of the legislature from '85 to '91 inclusive. J. C. Hollman's first session was in '83, and the veteran W. K. Sullivan has represented The Evening Journal "off and on" for many years. Sketches of late arrivals and several old friends are submitted below. At every session the legislative press gallery has been filled with conspicuously bright, able and untiring news-gatherers.

MR. HOLLMAN.

HOLLMAN, JOSEPH C., in charge of The Chicago Record Bureau is a native of southwestern Wisconsin, and was born in 1846. He learned the printer's trade in a country newspaper office, and with the exception of a brief service in the army, has been continuously in newspaper work since '60. He was typo and telegraph editor on the Milwaukee Sentinel from '66 to '74, and then accompanied a retiring proprietor of that journal to Quincy, Ill., where, during fourteen years, he served in every reportorial and editorial position on The Daily Whig. In the meantime he had become familiar with legislation and politics in Illinois, representing The Chicago Tribune in the lower house of the general assembly in '83 and being in attendance upon all subsequent sessions. In '88 he removed to Chicago and became a reporter on The Morning News now The Record and has since reported four sessions of the legislature for it and has done state politics during the campaigns.

MacMILLAN, THOMAS C., in charge of The Chicago Inter Ocean Bureau, was born at Stranraer, Scotland, Oct. 4, 1850, and in '57 moved with his parents to Chicago, where he attended the public schools for a time, leaving to serve as an apprentice to a machinist. Poor health compelled him to abandon this, and he returned to school, graduating from the high school. Then he entered the Chicago University. In January, '73, he became a reporter on The Inter Ocean. In '75 he went as correspondent of that paper with the Black Hills exploring expedition, and in '75-6 he represented his paper with Gen. Crook in his campaign against Sitting Bull and his hostile Sioux. In '78 he made an extensive tour of Europe and in '80 succeeded Robert P. Porter as editor of "Our Curiosity Shop," an important department of The Inter Ocean. In '82 he succeeded George B. Armstrong as city editor, and two years later returned to the "Curiosity Shop." In January, '83 he married Miss Mary C. Goudie of Na-au-say, Kendall county. He has served as a member of the Cook County Board of Education for three years and for five years has been secretary and director of the Chicago Free Kindergarten association, and is also a director of the American Educational Aid association of Illinois; was director for two terms in the Chicago Public Library. Mr. MacMillan was elected to the house in '84 and '86, and advanced to the senate in '88, his term

MR. MACMILLAN.

expiring in '92; he was named by the republicans for congress last year, but was defeated. He was a charter member of the Chicago Press Club, and is first vice president of the Illinois St. Andrews Society. In June, '85, Illinois College at Jacksonville conferred on him the degree of Master of Arts. He is a quiet, but energetic worker.

BURDETT, SAM M., in charge of The Chicago Herald Bureau, was born in Boyle county, Kentucky, February 5, 1854. He studied law and was admitted to the bar in '76. In '78 he was elected prosecuting attorney of Rockcastle county in his native state, holding the office for four years. While engaged in the practice of law he developed a taste for journalistic work, which he cultivated by making occasional contributions to the columns of The Louisville Courier-Journal. In '84 Mr. Burdett was given a position by Mr. Henry Watterson on the editorial staff of The Courier-Journal. In November, '87, he was appointed a special agent of the United States Internal Revenue department under President Cleveland and was assigned to duty in the northwest with headquarters at Omaha. He resigned the office of revenue agent soon after the accession of President Harrison and returned to Kentucky. March 24, '90, Mr. Burdett was married to Miss Clara B. Russell, daughter of A. A. Russell, of Massillon, Ohio. Immediately after his marriage he went with his wife to Denver, Col., where they resided for one year, removing to Chicago in May, '91. In the following August he was employed as an editorial writer on the

MR. BURDETT.

staff of The Chicago Herald, and last January Mr. Burdett was sent to Springfield and placed in charge of The Herald's legislative bureau.

GRAHAM, WILLIAM A. S., in charge of The Chicago Times Bureau, was born in Newtownhamilton, County Armagh, Ireland, Feb. 6, 1863, and received a good common school education. In '79 he came to America and was employed as office boy in The Philadelphia Press. Subsequently he became a copy-holder and graduated as a writer under the tutelage of Maj. Moses P. Handy, the present chief of the Bureau of Publicity and Promotion of the World's Fair. In '82 he

MR. GRAHAM.

went to Denver, and two years later moved to Chicago, prior to the democratic national convention of '84, and has been doing politics for Chicago newspapers ever since. He was with The Times in '84; The Tribune in '89, reporting the legislative session that year, and on the adjournment of the legislature was made secretary of the press bureau by the Chicago newspapers, and assigned to the task of working up sentiment through the press for Chicago as the world's fair city. At this time he was attacked with typhoid fever and nearly died. On recovering, he reported the special session of the legislature for The Herald, continuing with that journal until after the election of '90, and has since been with The Times. He had charge of the legislative bureau of that paper in '91, and in the campaign of '92 was a very valuable and discreet aid to Gov. Altgeld and the democratic ticket. His labors were recognized, for he was made commissioner of the Illinois & Michigan canal by the governor. He took an active interest in the campaign of Carter H. Harrison, editor of The Times, for mayor of Chicago this spring and was selected as private secretary to the mayor by Mr. Harrison, a position for which he is eminently qualified.

Jan. '88 he was married to Miss Caroline Brown, of Evanston, and they have had two boys, one of whom is living.

SULLIVAN, WILLIAM K., in charge of The Chicago Evening Journal Bureau, was born in Waterford, Ireland, Nov. 10, 1843. He was edu-

MR. SULLIVAN.

cated at the Waterford Model School and in Dublin. In his youth he was intended for a Methodist minister, but he preferred to seek his fortune in America and in another pursuit. He emigrated in '63, and his career for a time was somewhat varied. He served in the 141st Ill. Inf.; taught school for a time in Kane and Kendall counties; ran an engine in West Virginia during the oil excitement there. Then he went to Europe, and when he returned stopped in New York for a time, contributing to Gen. Halpin's (Miles O'Reilly) Citizen. Then he read proof and became a reporter on the New York Sun under Moses Beach, and served under Charles A. Dana before he returned to the west and Chicago. He was first connected with The Tribune, and afterwards The Evening Journal. He has been with this reliable chronicler of events for eighteen years as city editor, managing editor and correspondent. He was a representative in the 27th General Assembly; was appointed by Mayor Colvin on the Chicago Board of Education, and served three years, two years as president of the board; was United States consul to the Bermudas during President Harrison's administration, and resigned in Oct. '92. In '64 he was married to Miss Amelia Shackelford, of Evanston, and has one son and one daughter. Mr. Sullivan has been on duty at every Illinois legislative assembly for over twenty years, and is almost as well known as the state house to public men of both parties.

JONES, ALEXANDER J., in charge of the Associated Press Bureau, was born in Sangamon Co., Ill., July 11, 1860. He was raised on a farm, and in 1877 entered the United States Naval Academy at Annapolis, on the nomination of Congressman Wm. M. Springer, as a cadet midshipman. After one year's service he resigned and, proceeding to London, shipped aboard a merchant vessel as seaman for Australia. He spent several months in Australia, traversing extensively the provinces of Victoria and New South Wales. Then he shipped at Sydney as an ordinary seaman on a Bolivian vessel for San Francisco. After two years' absence, and having sailed around the world as sailor before the mast, he returned to Illinois, and in '80 began teaching school. Three years later he entered the newspaper business, spending two years in France and other European countries to perfect his knowledge in literature and acquire proficiency in the French language. In '84-5-6 he was employed successively on The New York Tribune, The Chicago Times and The Chicago

MR. JONES.

Inter Ocean, finally going to Washington as clerk of the Committee on Claims of the house of representatives. He was married in '85 to Miss Agnes S. Chalmers, of Springfield, Ill., and they have one child, a boy. In '88 he was appointed by President Cleveland as United States consul at Barranquilla, Colombia, South America and held this office until the expiration of the Cleveland administration. He then returned to the newspaper profession accepting a position on The Chicago Times, and finally became the manager of the Springfield Legislative Bureau of the Associated Press in '89. For the past four years he has been the political correspondent of the Associated Press and has reported nearly all the great events, political and otherwise, in the United States since that time, including the Johnstown horror, the Cronin trial, the Homestead riots, many state conventions, and three national conventions. During the sessions of the last congress he represented the Associated Press at Washington, D. C., returning to Springfield every alternate year to take charge of the Illinois Legislative Bureau.

FITZMAURICE, D. C., in charge of The St. Louis Republic Bureau at the sessions of '91-'93, was born in Cincinnati, May 12, 1855. His early education was in the schools of Illinois, at Kansas and Charleston, and completed by taking the full course at Hughes' High School, Cincinnati. His first newspaper work was on The Cincinnati Star, then a new daily pa-

MR. FITZMAURICE.

per, since consolidated with The Times. Later he was on the local staff of The Cincinnati Enquirer. In June, '76, he took the editorial management of a new democratic daily which the democrats of Alton were anxious to establish after several failures by men who have since become eminent in journalism, politics and commerce. The first number of The Alton Democrat appeared under his management June 17, '76, and he remained the editor of the paper for twelve years. In '88 he contributed a series of letters to The St. Louis Republic, developing the practical operation of the taxation and revenue sys-

MR. KIDD.

tems of Illinois. After the close of the campaign of that year he was attached to the staff of The Republic as staff correspondent. In that capacity he has seen wide and varied service in all parts of the country.

KIDD, THOMAS W. S., editor and proprietor of The Daily Monitor, of Springfield, was born in New Castle, Del., Oct. 22, 1828. His parents were natives of Delaware, but of Irish descent. Both Capt. Kidd's parents died when he was very young, and he was raised by an aunt. He attended school but six weeks during his life. In '40 the family moved to Philadelphia and Thomas served two years as errand boy in a merchant tailoring establishment. Here T. S. Arthur and other literary celebrities frequently met and young Kidd in listening to their conversation first conceived the idea of learning something of books and the world. He learned the trades of printer and stereotyper and subsequently that of blacksmith and machinist, and was with locomotive builders at Wilmington until '49, when he removed to Chicago and took charge of extensive iron shops. He soon tired of this and accepted a place as traveling agent for an agricultural implement firm, remaining in this line until '57. In

February, '56, he moved to Springfield; in '57 was bailiff in the U. S. marshal's office; in '58 was elected coroner and appointed deputy sheriff; in the winters of '58-'59 and '59-'60 he served as sheriff of the Supreme Court; in '60 he was made crier of the U. S. District Court by Judge Treat, which he held until '77; he was assessor of Springfield for fifteen years and collector for two years; in '58 he read law and was admitted to the bar. He established the Sangamo Monitor May 1, '73 and The Morning Monitor June 28, '77. In July, '54, he married Miss Charlotte Janney, of Cecil Co., Md., and six children have been born to them, of whom one a daughter survives. As a writer Capt. Kidd has a peculiar style of his own. He uses very plain English without frills and everybody knows what he means.

MR. DAVIS.

DAVIS, JOHN McCAN, in charge of The St. Louis Globe-Democrat Bureau, is a native of Fulton County, this state. His first journalistic experience was in Canton, Ill., where he was engaged in newspaper work for several years. He came to Springfield in '88 and connected himself with The Illinois State Journal. He has been in charge of the legislative work of The Globe-Democrat for two sessions—the Thirty-seventh and Thirty-eighth General Assemblies. Mr. Davis, at different times, has represented a number of metropolitan papers at the state capital, being now the resident correspondent of The Chicago Times and several eastern papers, including The New York World. He represents several journals.

MITCHELL, HENRY ROBLY, representing several prominent dailies, was born in Illinois and was educated as a practical farmer. He entered the United States service at the

MR. MITCHELL.

age of twenty years, and since the war has been engaged in newspaper work of different kinds. For the past fifteen years he has been connected with The Chicago Inter Ocean most of the time, and has been a reporter in the Illinois legislature since the memorable Logan-Morrison contest in 1885.

VAUGHN, JOHN E., in charge of The Springfield Morning Monitor, was born in Belleville, Ill., Sept. 17, 1870. He received a good

MR. VAUGHN.

common school education in the Belleville schools. He came to Springfield about six years ago, and began on The Monitor as police and justices' courts reporter, and made this department of The Monitor a feature of the paper. He reported the legislature of '91 and was assigned to "do" the state conventions and local and state politics for Capt. Kidd's aggressive journal. He did his work well, and is a reliable and able reporter and writer. He is the youngest correspondent in charge of the work for any newspaper this session. The Monitor publishes the best and most comprehensive reports of the legislative proceedings of any local paper.

PICKERING, JOHN L., of Springfield, who has represented various metropolitan papers during legislative sessions, and is the compiler of this book, was born near Neoga, Ill., Sept. 12, 1860, and spent his boyhood in Arcola. In '75 he was train boy on the Illinois Central, and afterwards switched to the position of brakeman

MR. PICKERING.

on a freight train, which he followed a year or more. He started to learn the printer's trade when 10 years old, and in '78 quit railroading for a "slug" in The Peoria National Democrat office, attending the Peoria high school at the same time. In '80-'82 he solicited subscribers for The Chicago Herald throughout the northwest, and worked as news compositor in the same office. Reported the legislature of '83 and '85 for The Springfield Register, and was telegraph editor of the same paper for several years. In '87 he established in Springfield a politico-society weekly, The Capital Idea, which he conducted for three years, and then sold it. He has contributed letters on Illinois politics since '84 to The Herald, The Times, The Republic and The Tribune; during the campaigns of '86, '88 and '90 was connected with The Herald and The Republic, and was with The Tribune in '92; was on The Times staff during the sessson of '91, and went on the Washington staff of that paper in Dec. '91. He is a practical printer in all departments. In Dec. '83, he married Miss Etta Rountree, of Nashville, Ill., and they have three children, a boy and two girls.

GRAIN INSPECTION.

In '71 the legislature passed laws providing for state inspection of grain in Chicago and placing it under the supervision of the railroad and warehouse commission. The grain inspection and warehouse registrar departments of Chicago were organized in July, '71, and since then the following have been chief inspectors: W. F. Tompkins, W. H. Harper, J. C. Smith, J. P. Reynolds, P. Bird Price and George P. Bunker. The chief inspector is appointed by the governor. The registrar is appointed by the railroad and warehouse commission, and the following have filled the office since '71: Stephen Clary, T. H. Tyndale, B. F. Culver, H. S. Dean, P. Bird Price, J. W. Burst, J. M. Turnbull and Louis Wagner. Messrs. Bunker and Wagner are the only officers of democratic faith that ever filled these positions. Although new to the duties they have given satisfactory ovidence of the wisdom of Gov. Altgeld in selecting them.

BUNKER, GEORGE P., Chief Grain Inspector, although active in politics for a number of years, is a successful business man. For fifteen years he has been a manufacturer of vinegar and pickles. In all the political campaigns in Chicago during the last seven years he has been a member of the executive committee of the county central committee, in every case acting as treasurer. The only political position he has held was that of alderman from the Eighth ward. He was for two years in the council and two years ago refused the office for a second term. Mr. Bunker was born in Franklin county, New York, forty-three years ago and at the age of eighteen moved to Chicago. The second day after his arrival he became a conductor on the West Division railway and remained there about a year. He then secured employment with William Goldie & Co., contractors, and was with that firm five years, when he embarked in the pickle and vinegar business. His abilities as a business man are unques-

GEO. P BUNKER.

tioned, and while in the council he served his ward and the city well. Mr. Bunker is a member of the Iroquois Club, and the Cook County Democracy and Marching Club.

WAGNER, LOUIS, Warehouse Registrar, was born in Watertown, Wis., Jan. 28, 1858, and has lived in Chicago since '66. He was educated at Northwestern University, Watertown, at Concordia Gymnasium, Fort Wayne, graduating in '76, and at Concordia

LOUIS WAGNER.

(Saxon) University, St. Louis, graduating in '79. He has been editor of German daily papers in St. Louis and Chicago for ten years. In '90 he was nominated for the state senate by the democrats of the Seventh district, and was defeated by only 833 votes, although his opponent was a prominent republican, and had been elected in '86 by a majority of over 2,300. Mr. Wagner made a tour of the state last year, speaking at forty-five places in English, German and Low German, for the democratic ticket. He devoted himself principally to exposing the iniquities of the Edwards Compulsory School Law, and is the author of the pamphlet, "A Brief History of the Edwards Law," a tract that provoked a great deal of newspaper controversy, and was circulated as a campaign document. He was appointed warehouse registrar March 13, 1893, a selection that was well received in the state.

PHOTOGRAPHER ANDERSON.

ANDERSON, L. S., the well known Springfield photographer, was born in Madison Co., N. Y., April 30, 1847, and received a good common school education. He came to Northern Illinois with his parents in '52, and spent most of his time until '67 in Rockford, where he learned his profession. He commenced business in '69 and has had a very successful experience. He established a studio in Springfield in '74, and in '84 was compelled to remove to larger quarters to his present location, north side of the square on account of increased business. He has negatives for every legislator since and including '85, when he made the Logan "103" group under contract with that statesman's friends. He keeps up with the latest improvements in his line, and that insures him the best trade.

SPECIAL COMMITTEES.

Joint committee to investigate the "sweat shop" evil—Senators Noonan (chairman), Mahoney and Chapman; Representatives O'Donnell, Dearborn, Deneen and May.

Joint committee to investigate the Whisky Trust — Senators Salomon (chairman), Evans and Mahoney; Representatives Smith of Livingston, McInerney, Carlin, Paddock and Cherry.

Joint committee to ascertain what additional accommodations are needed for the Appellate Court, First district —Senators Johnson (chairman), O'Malley and Humphrey; Representatives Donnelly, McInerney and O'Connell.

Senate committee to investigate charges against the former management of the Joliet penitentiary—Senators Green (chairman), O'Conor, Allen, Arnold, Manecke, Bacon and Howell.

Senate committee to investigate the School Book and School Furniture Trusts—Senators Arnold (chairman), Noonan, Ford, O'Malley, Ferguson, Mussett and Humphrey.

House committee to investigate the "Big Four" railroad wreck at Wann—Representatives Fowler (chairman), McMillan, Snyder, Baldwin, Caughlan, Fletcher, Snedeker.

HOLD-OVER SENATORS.

The following state senators were elected in 1892 and hold over during the session of 1895:
Aspinwall, rep., Stephenson.
Barnes, dem., Marshall.
Bartling, dem., Cook.
Berry, rep., Hancock.
Bogardus, rep., Ford.
Brands, dem., Randolph.
Campbell, dem., Hamilton.
Coon, rep., Lake.
Craig, dem., Coles.
Dunlap, rep., Champaign.
Evans, rep., Kane.
Ford, dem., Clinton.
Green, dem., Alexander.
Hamer, rep., Fulton.
Higbee, dem., Pike.
Howell, rep., McLean.
Hunter, rep., Winnebago.
Johnson, dem., Cook.
Leeper, dem., Cass.
Letourneau, rep., Kankakee.
Mussett, rep., Edwards.
Niehaus, dem., Peoria.
Paisley, dem., Montgomery.
Salomon, dem., Cook.
Wall, dem., Macoupin.

The re-apportionment of senatorial districts will not affect the position of the above senators. They are all from even-numbered districts, and are divided politically 14 democrats and 11 republicans.

MEMBERS RETURNED.

The following members of the present General Assembly were members of the legislature of 1891:

Senators—
Berry,
Bogardus,
Campbell,
Craig,
Evans,
Green,
Hamer,
Higbee,
Hunt,
Leeper.

Representatives—
Anderson, J. O.,
Armstrong,
Barton,
Beals,
Berry,
Bryan,
Burke,
Callahan,
Carmody,
Carson,
Cherry,
Conway,
Crafts,
Dearborn,
Donnelly,
Duncan,
Ellsworth,
Erickson,
Farrell,
Ferns,
Forsythe,
Griggs,
Hawley,
Hopkins,
Kelly,
Kwasigroch,
Lyman,
McCrone,
McInerney,
May,
Merritt,
Meyer, Ernst,
Myers,
Nohe,
O'Connell,
O'Donnell,
O'Loughlin,
Paddock,
Payne,
Preston,
Reed,
Rohrer,
Smith, J. A.,
Smith, W. S.,
Spellman,
Straight,
Stringer,
Talbot,
Thiemann,
Tice,
Warder.
Watson,
Wilke,
Wilson, J. P.,
Wiwi,
—65.

This is the first General Assembly since that of 1881 that has not chosen a United States Senator. Shelby M. Cullom was elected in 1883 to succeed David Davis. John A. Logan was elected in 1885 to succeed himself after a four months' battle royal with Wm. R. Morrison. In 1887 Charles B. Farwell was chosen to succeed Gen. Logan who died in 1886. Senator Cullom was re-elected in 1889, and in 1891 John M. Palmer broke the republican record.

STATE OFFICERS.

Governor..................................John P. Altgeld, Dem., Chicago
Lieutenant-Governor................Joseph B. Gill, Dem., Murphysboro
Secretary of State...............William H. Hinrichsen, Dem., Jacksonville
State Treasurer........................Rufus N. Ramsay, Dem., Carlyle
Attorney General.....................Maurice T. Maloney, Dem., Ottawa
Superintendent of Public Instruction..........Henry Raab, Dem., Belleville
Auditor of Public Accounts.................David Gore, Dem., Carlinville
Private Secretary to Governor............Wm. F. Dose, Dem., Chicago

SENATE OFFICERS AND EMPLOYES.

PRESIDENT............................Joseph B. Gill, Murphysboro
PRESIDENT PRO TEM................John W. Coppinger, Alton
SECRETARY..........................Finis E. Downing, Virginia
  First Assistant..................................E. P. Kimball, Virden
  Second Assistant...............................R. S. Bayne, Varna
Reading Clerk......................Mrs. Phocion Howard, Danville
President's Private Secretary..............C. D. Tufts, Centralia
Enrolling and Engrossing Clerk...........Fred J. Kern, Belleville
  First Assistant..............................Harvey J. Jones, Carlyle
  Second Assistant.........................Gerhart Weber, Hillsboro
Sergeant-at-Arms....................Robert H. Davis, Carrollton
  First Assistant...............................Edwin Bowen, Decatur
  Second Assistant..........................Robert Welch, Chicago
Chaplain........................Rev. Dr. F. W. Taylor, Springfield
Postmaster.........................Mrs. M. O'Conner, Springfield
  Assistant Postmaster...................Miss Mary Turner, Mattoon
Superintendent of Ventilation...........................J. E. Judy
  Assistant................................W. H. Duckstein, Springfield

HOUSE OFFICERS AND EMPLOYES.

SPEAKER...........................Clayton E. Crafts, Chicago
CLERK..................................Rob't W. Ross, Vandalia
  First Assistant...............................W. E. Handy, Tolono
  Second Assistant...........................W. B. Morris, Golconda
  Third Assistant...........................James E. Vail, Macomb
Bill Clerk.......................H. B. Lichtenberger, Freeport
Custodian of Printed Bills............Chas. T. Bouillon, Carlinville
Doorkeeper............................E. S. Browne, Mendota
  First Assistant.........................John N. Summers, Chicago
  Second Assistant...................John McDarrah, Rock Island
  Third Assistant..........................B. W. Rives, Kankakee
Enrolling and Engrossing Clerk............A. E. Simonson, Dixon
  First Assistant.............................Adam Gard, Marshall
  Second Assistant...................Louis I. Hutchins, Keithsburg
Postmaster........................Miss Mollie McCabe, Springfield
  Asssistant....................Miss Kathryn Gallagher, Springfield
Chaplain........................Rev. Joseph Hawkins, Lincoln
Speaker's Private Secretary..............Will E. McGurren, Chicago
Press Messenger....................George R. Berriman, Springfield
Superintendent of Ventilation..............Theodore Adelman, Alton
Chief Page........................Phocion Howard, Jr., Danville

NAFEW, JOHN A., chief clerk of the St. Nicholas Hotel, and one of the most popular and best known men in Illinois, was born in Troy, N. Y., Sept. 17, 1837, and is the oldest son of John S. and Mary H. (Weaver) Nafew. He received a common school education, and began life as a druggist in Albany, continuing it for four years. In '55 he moved to Chicago, and soon afterwards to Wisconsin, where he clerked in a hotel for a year. For three years he was clerk of the old Pike House, Bloomington, Ill., and in '60 he entered the office of the St. Nicholas, at Springfield, remaining until '65, when he was made general ticket agent of the Jeffersonville railroad. In two years he returned to the St. Nicholas, and then took charge of the American House, which he ran acceptably for three years, and returned to the old reliable St. Nicholas, where he has been ever since. In '63 he married Miss E. Frank McIntire, of Springfield, and one daughter has been born to them. He is a Royal Arch Chapter Mason; was master workman in Lodge 37, A. O. U. W., for two years and has been a member of the Hotel Men's association for years. December 17, '92, his friends among the traveling public and guests of the St. Nicholas complimented his uniform courtesy and efforts to please by tendering him a complimentary banquet, at which he was presented with a handsome watch charm of virgin gold, in tablet form, with large star set in diamonds. On the tablets were engraved the names of about fifty friends of Mr. Nafew.

CHIEF CLERK NAFEW.

MAIN DINING ROOM, ST. NICHOLAS HOTEL.

ITALIAN MARBLE STATUE, CUT FROM PHOTO, BY RICHTER & DOLAND, ARTISTIC MONUMENTS, SPRINGFIELD.

THE CAPITOL.

LADIES' PARLORS, LELAND HOTEL.

THE LINCOLN MONUMENT.

OUTFITTERS TO THE STATESMEN OF ILLINOIS.

EXECUTIVE MANSION — GOV. ALTGELD'S RESIDENCE.

THE LINCOLN HOME.

PRINCIPAL DINING ROOM, LELAND HOTEL.

THE OLD STATE CAPITOL.—PRESENT SANGAMON COUNTY COURT HOUSE.

LEGISLATIVE SOUVENIR.

BETTIE STUART INSTITUTE.—A DAY AND BOARDING SCHOOL FOR YOUNG LADIES AND CHILDREN. MRS. A. M. BROOKS, PRINCIPAL. SEND FOR CATALOGUE.

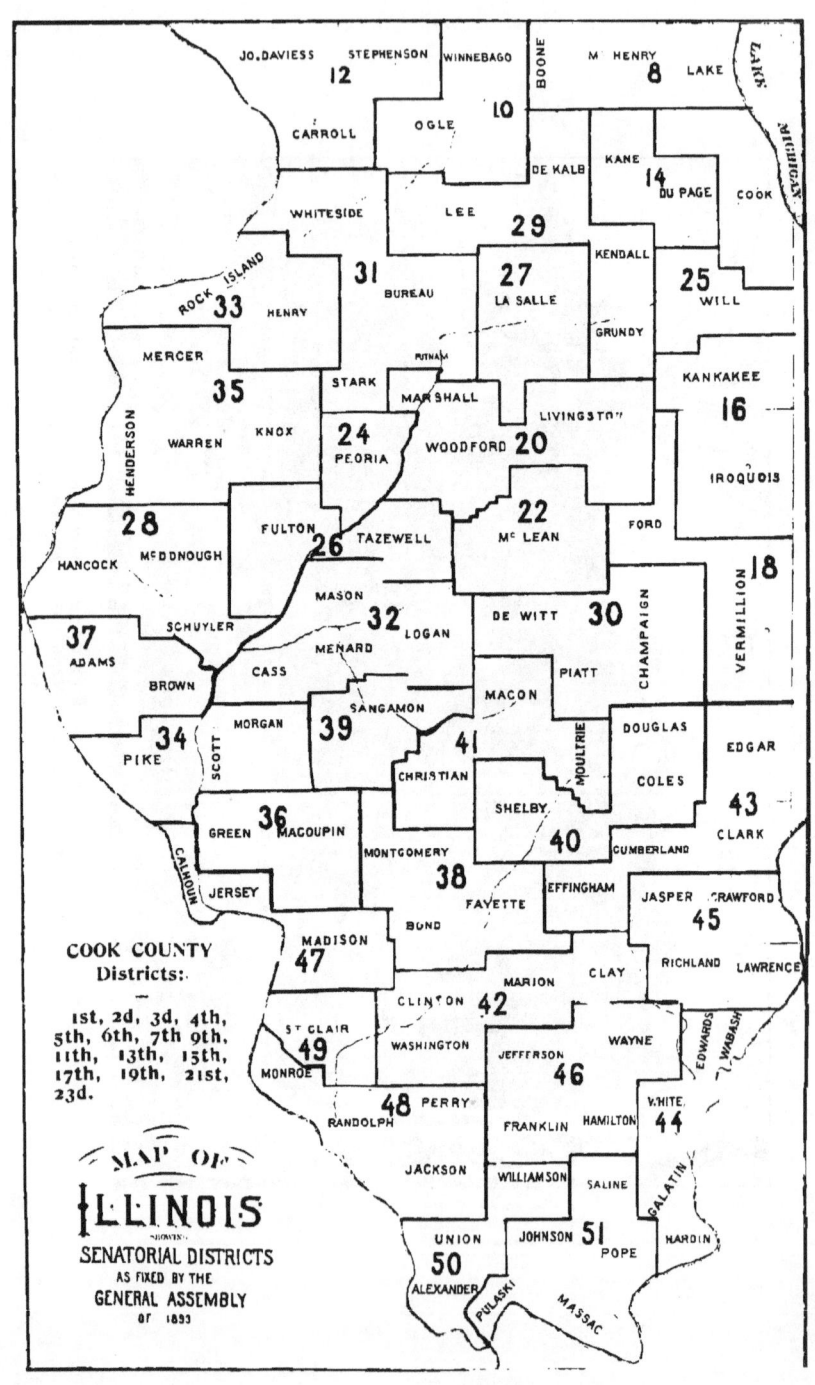

ILLINOIS BUILDING, WORLD'S FAIR.

INDEX

STATE OFFICERS—
Altgeld, John P. 4
Gill, Joseph B. 5
Hinrichsen, William H. 6
Maloney, Maurice T. 9
Raab, Henry 8
Ramsay, Rufus N. 7

THE SENATE—
Davis, Robert H., Sergeant-at-Arms 17
Downing, Finis E., Secretary 17
Taylor, Rev. Dr. F. W., Chaplain 38
Senators, arranged alphabetically, beginning 18

THE HOUSE—
Browne, Edgar S., Doorkeeper 42
Crafts, Clayton E., Speaker 39
Ross, Robert W., Clerk 41
Representatives, arranged alphabetically, beginning 42

OTHER SKETCHES—
Freeman, Norman L., Reporter Supreme Court 11
Hereford, Arthur L., Printer Expert 15
Jones, George W., Clerk Appellate Court 12
Orendorff, Alfred, Adjutant General 10
Paddock, James H., Ex-Secretary Railroad Commissioners 15
Snively, Ethan A., Clerk Supreme Court 12

RAILROAD AND WAREHOUSE COMMISSIONERS—
Cantrell, William S., Chairman of Board 13
Gahan, Thomas 14
Lape, Charles F. 13
Yantis, John W., Secretary 14
Bunker, George P., Chief Grain Inspector 99
Wagner, Louis, Registrar 100

THE PRESS GALLERY—
Burdett, Sam. M. 95
Davis, J. McCan 98
Hollman, J. C. 94
Fitzmaurice, D. C. 97
Graham, W. A. S. 95
Jones, A. J. 96
Kidd, T. W. S. 97
MacMillan, T. C. 94
Mitchell, H. R. 98
Pickering, J. L. 99
Sullivan, W. K. 96
Vaughn, J. E. 98

MATTERS OF INTEREST—
Brief mention of past newspaper correspondents 93
Hold-over Senators 101
House officers, List of 102
List of Chief Grain Inspectors and Registrars 99
Map showing new senatorial districts 114
Members Returned in 1892 101
Representatives, compensation, etc 41
Special Committees, Joint and Senate and House 101
Senate officers, List of 102
Senators, compensation, etc 17
State officers, List of 102
Steering committees, Senate and House 41
The general assembly, facts in regard to 17

www.ingramcontent.com/pod-product-compliance
Lightning Source LLC
Chambersburg PA
CBHW031401160426
43196CB00007B/847